A BRIEF HISTORY OF
SAUGERTIES

A BRIEF HISTORY OF SAUGERTIES

MICHAEL SULLIVAN SMITH

THE History PRESS

Published by The History Press
Charleston, SC
www.historypress.net

Cover images courtesy of the Saugerties Public Library local history room collections.

First published 2016

Manufactured in the United States

ISBN 978.1.46713.594.8

Library of Congress Control Number: 2016930885

CONTENTS

ACKNOWLEDGEMENTS

I am grateful to all those individuals and organizations that have graciously made available the collections and artifacts so crucial to awareness of this history. Most greatly appreciated are the insights of Audrey Klinkenberg in her many roles, including town historian, associate county historian, DAR registrar and genealogical society president, but mostly for her untiring labors as transcriber of the many handwritten ledgers, minute books, letter books and diaries I have scanned and she has made searchable digitally. Without these now accessible in the library along with the many other research resources she has assembled, the character of the times found in this work would be missing and the book would be lifeless.

Also I am thankful to Judge Daniel N. Lamb Jr. for the unrestricted access to everything Morris Rosenblum left at 41 Market Street. Dan's encouragement of the organizing and interpretation of this priceless legacy and his allowing it to become an attraction to all those open to discussing Saugerties history has raised the consciousness of this community.

I am thoroughly indebted to Chester Hartwell and every contributor to his I Like Saugerties Facebook page over the past half decade. His efforts have driven a popular interest in Saugerties history forward. Chester's questions and dedication to the graphic interpretation of local history material both from Saugerties and the broader region has inspired a new wave of history lovers, and that, in turn, has inspired me.

I am lastly, but most profoundly, in humble and devoted acknowledgment of the late Jean Wrolsen, who emptied her personal library so I may have what was precious and rare twenty-five years ago, for giving me her space in the *Post Star* to exercise weekly summations of my knowledge and, lastly, for enshrining my early, meager writings with the volumes of works created and collected by her for the local history room of the Saugerties Public Library it has since dedicated to her memory.

PROLOGUE

The decade after World War II changed Saugerties. The bright prospects of the Thruway shook its confidence to the core.

Its focus had turned toward Kingston. Just as in its earliest history, it became dependent on the attention of a powerful corporate neighbor.

Saugerties embraced a new identity as a subordinate neighborhood. Housing developments, a doubling population and massive investments in schools and public facilities were all in the works, committing its future to that of a commuter community.

Saugerties' traditional values and its legacy identity were hollowed out. In this new role, its century-old estates and mills became blocked from memory.

Then the object of this change vanished. Confused, Saugerties couldn't shake an illusion it had embraced and continued justifying its purpose by identifying with amenities created to support a now lost function.

Institutional Saugerties had forgotten that for better than a century before this it was self-sufficient. It still, today, continues to ignore the significance of that, thinking its historic identity prevents it from being competitive for the attention it lost.

Yet everything considered attractive in today's world was historically here. Saugerties' history is one of seasoned entrepreneurial managers, the active owners of a long line of businesses, guiding its success for their own good and for that of the community.

There is scarcely anything left in today's Saugerties that can prepare one for comprehending what functioned as commerce, society, intellectual exchange and capital in the history of Saugerties. Historic Saugerties was closer to what is branded a Silicon Valley—today's gold standard of economic security. Actually, even that allusion can't hold a candle to the story hidden in the midst of Saugerties' past.

Saugerties' historic identity is the information every citizen and seeker of the presence of an inspirational story needs. That whole story will appear in these pages, from the beginnings that go back to the Native Americans and Dutch to factual details discovered in this age of more total access to records than has ever existed in the past.

Aerial photographs taken just as International Business Machines Corporation (IBM) was about to open (and its suburbanization of Saugerties double the population) show a neighborhood around mills that the last quarter of the twentieth century derogatorily called "the gut." This photographic reminder introduces a past almost totally forgotten today.

This *gut* word for the land that the mills once covered was *gat*, a Dutch word for cut or ravine, and was long used to describe this land feature. The Dutch farmers and even the Native Americans for their plantations all favored the heights of the level land cut in two by this ravine. The mills' use of nature's waters flowing through that lower place was never fully valued by the general population—thus "gut." But this gat is, in actuality, the womb of Saugerties' history.

When Henry Barclay bought the farm of Tjerck Schoonmaker to flood the gat for a millpond, a farmhouse and a large barn occupied the rim of Barclay Heights. They hugged the edge of the bank there not for the fine view out over the river and mountains but just not to take up any of the precious level land that provided the only livelihood known before Barclay's arrival. The land below is what interested Henry Barclay, land of no use for anything but grazing sheep. Even its stone was too hard to quarry and use for building.

All the land between where the deep ravine of the Esopus Creek flows into the Hudson River and down past Glasco was held onto by the Natives longer than anywhere else along the river. This was *Tendeyachmeck* in their language, which translates to "Flatbush," an indicator of the deep clay that only the hardiest of scrub managed a stunted growth in. This was of little interest to the early Dutch who sought river- and creek-side land for their planting. The first Europeans to settle in Saugerties had their homestead in the gat, below this flatbush land, where silt from floods refreshed the soil.

That first settler, John Wood, had his homestead at the Esopus bend. This was before 1687, the year George Meales and Richard Hayes claimed that

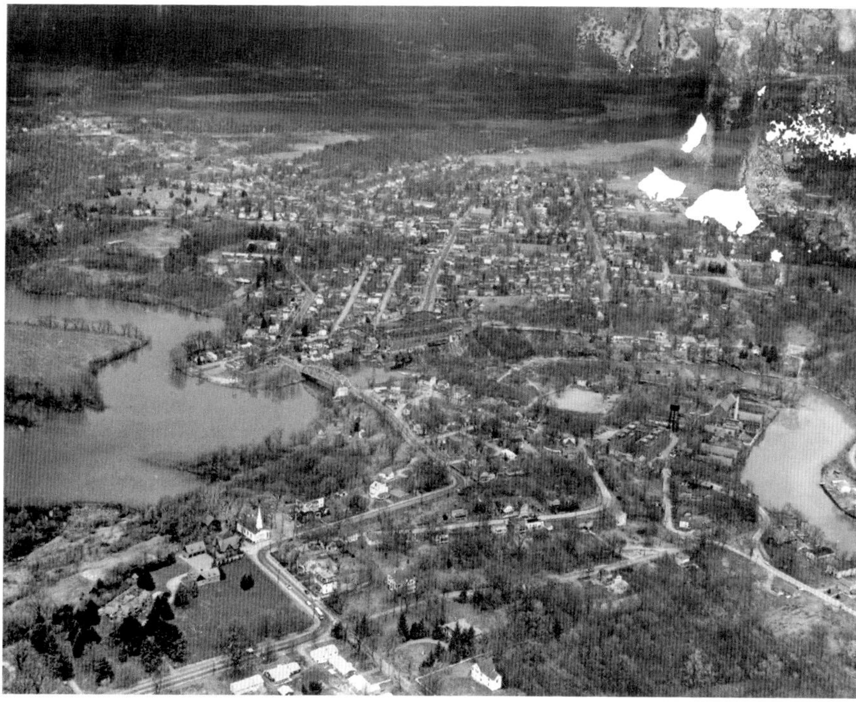

The mills deep in the Esopus ravine as seen from over Barclay Heights in a village view from the early 1960s. *R&L Archive collection.*

land in a patent. They sold John Wood the land he had settled on, making his presence here the first to be recorded. He is plainly here before that deed because all his improvements are itemized in its record.

One item recorded is a sawmill. The Native Americans had their Tendeyachmeck lands taken away in the Andros Treaty ten years earlier in 1677, and John Wood and his wife, Hannah, may well have arrived at that time or shortly before. In the Andros Treaty, there is an exception by the Native Americans to a settler who was a sawyer they had already traded land to. They describe this land as under the hills. That could have been referencing this land in the ravine below what is called the Plantesie Berg.

John Persen bought the part of the Meales and Hayes Patent north of the Esopus gat in 1712. He had a mill where Martin Cantine, in the first years of the twentieth century, placed his hydroelectric wheelhouse. The old lead mill pictured in *The Pearl* in ruins in 1875 was there. When Henry Barclay created the millpond, it backed the water over the second falls upstream

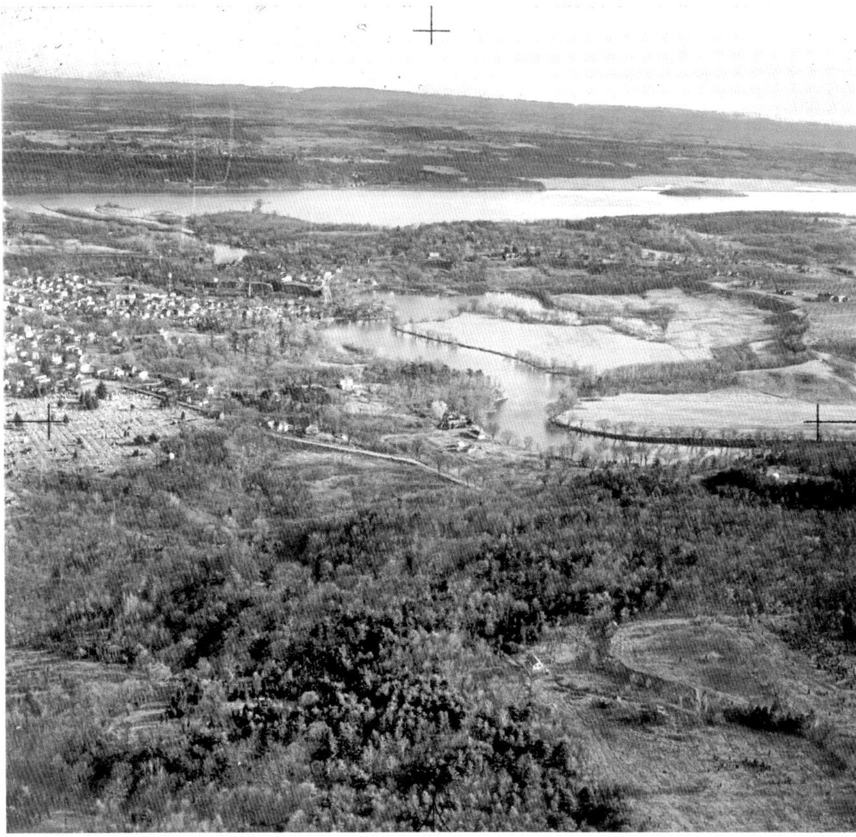

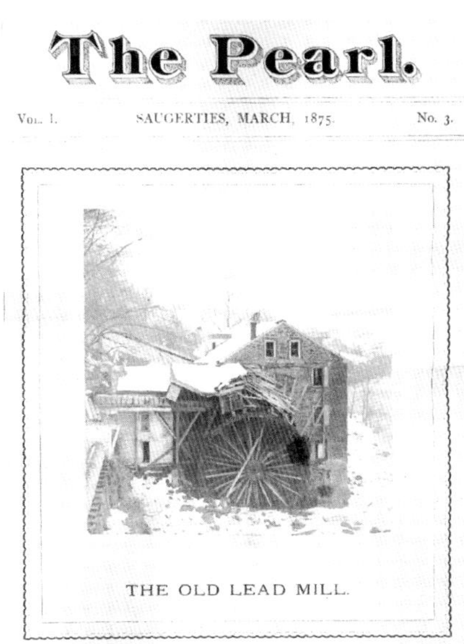

The Pearl.

Vol. I. SAUGERTIES, MARCH, 1875. No. 3.

THE OLD LEAD MILL.

Above: The Esopus bends under the Plantesie Berg toward the Hudson into the millpond raised behind Henry Barclay's 1825 dam. *R&L Archive collection.*

Left: The mills and the waterworks that powered them are already romanticized in an 1875 image of an early Industrial Revolution ruin. *Courtesy Audrey Klinkenberg.*

where John Wood's mill would have stood. Mills are marked there on a map made by John Kiersted in 1825, before Barclay's dam.

Only incidental events common to any other history of early settlement happened in Saugerties before the arrival of Henry Barclay. A classified advertisement in the *New York Evening Post* of February 2, 1826, is the earliest introduction to him:

> *Valuable site for Manufactories at Saugerties*
> *The Woodstock and Saugerties General Manufacturing and Mining Co. offer for sale or lease, on highly advantageous terms, Lots and Mill privileges of any description, for manufacturing purposes, with water power as may be wanted from 6 inches to 50 cubic feet: also, one thousand building lots, handsomely situated, to accommodate actual settlers, or persons who may purchase, or rent the water lots. Saugerties is pleasantly situated in Ulster country, 110 miles from the city of New-York, in a high and healthy country, on the west bank of the Hudson River, on the state road from Albany to New York, commanding fine views of the Catskill mountains and the Hudson River. Its contiguity to the mountains, is favourable for supplies of timber and fuel. The high state of cultivation of the lands in the neighbourhood of Saugerties, and the populous settlements of respectable and industrious farmers, will insure a low price of labour and provisions. The present price of boarding labourers is one dollar fifty cents per week. The price of transportation to and from New York is fifty cents per ton. There are on and near the premises, excellent stone quarries, clay, limestone and sand for building. The creek water is pure and soft, being supplied with springs on the mountains. There are also several springs of the purest and softest water, well calculated for cleaning woollen goods, rags, &c. for Paper Mills—which may be conveniently fed to the upper stories of the manufactories. Several extensive Manufactories of Iron. Paper. Calico Printing, &c. are far advanced and will be put into full operation this year. The contiguity to the city of New York, and facility of passing by sloops or steam boats; the quantity of water——healthiness of climate and low price of transportation, are among the numerous advantages of Saugerties, over any other manufacturing town in the United States. The price of tide water lots of convenient size, with one cubic foot of water to be drawn with a head of eighteen inches, and a fall of twenty-five feet on tide water of sufficient depth for vessels drawing 10 feet water, will be $500 per annum. Lots equally well situated 900 to 300 yards from tide water, with the same head and fall, will be from 300 to 400 per cubic foot par annum. The fee*

of the lots may be purchased at a reasonable rate, if wanted for immediate improvement, liberal inducements will be offered to companies, who may wish to make extensive manufacturing establishments.

Inquire of HENRY BARCLAY. President of said Company, at Saugerties, or of EZRA WEEKS, New York. a3 tf

The first assessment roll for Saugerties on which Henry Barclay appears is for 1827. There are 412 property owners with 104 structures for a total valuation of $300,000 in the entire town. When the minutes of the first decade of the Village of Ulster trustees was transcribed, many of the names of officials and residents in the 1830s were those who appeared on this 1827 record. From this it may be assumed that Henry Barclay's industrialization reinforced a population that was here far before his arrival with its economy developed as an agrarian community.

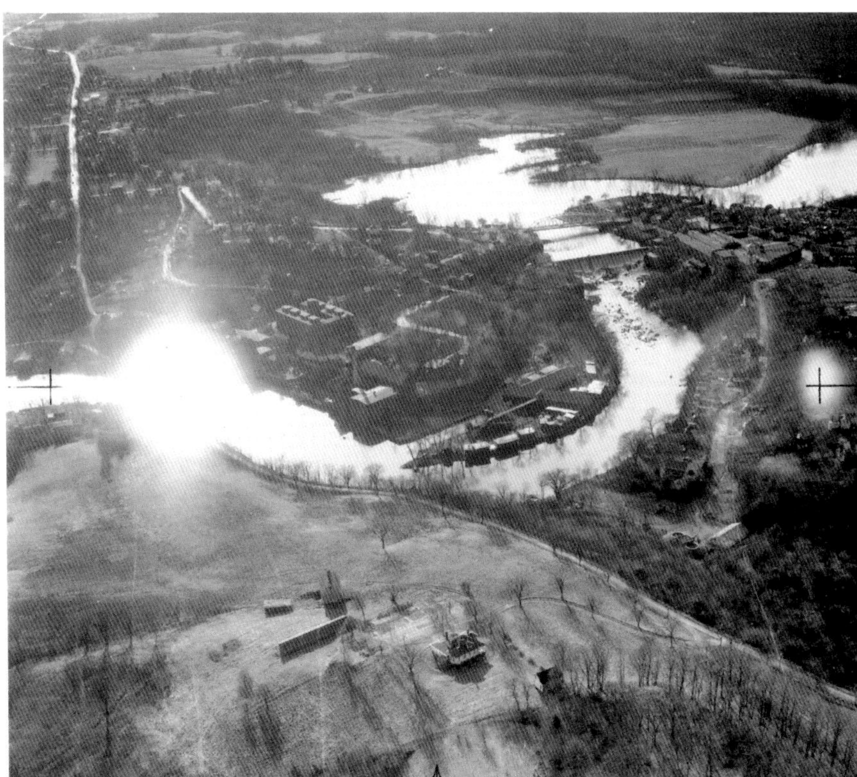

The mills of Saugerties seen from over open fields in the 1950s are all gone today, and the fields are covered by housing. *R&L Archive collection.*

This brief history of Saugerties has two parallel universes that shared a plan based on a natural situation as a hub of transportation. This was retained throughout its entire early industrial development in a coordinated economy of both the resources of the countryside and industrialization.

These two parallel universes in Saugerties are what make its history interesting. The industrial side attracted the attention, and even after its decline, the countryside continued reaping the benefits of that attraction, simply transitioning with the changing times to support the resorts, boardinghouses and seasonal colonies of the pre–World War II years. Supporting the industrial base and supporting those who visited here were one and the same.

But it is the industrial past and all the innovative ideas it attracted here over nearly two centuries that is historically significant. So this brief history centers on the Saugerties with this above-standard early Industrial Revolution history of successes in a population that never really successfully adapted to that identity.

This is changing with our times. Right now, history is what water power was nearly two centuries ago. To the innovators and thinkers who look at Saugerties, history is a prime asset. As history here makes clear, Saugerties is not a place but a presence. It is not a presence of buildings and land as much as it is one of man's sculpting of the earth to leave lasting historical connections.

This inspirational idea first surfaces in the postwar years when a short list of figures who recognized our historical connections to this legacy of the land appear. Morris Rosenblum, as one, approached this thought and had the intelligence, education and experience required to revel in it.

Morris carried a perspective that few could fathom before or after him. As a young lawyer in New York at the height of the Depression, Morris dealt with old industries struggling with bankruptcy. He knew the complexities of Saugerties' industrial history well before setting up a practice here in 1935. His love for aerial photography that he brought back from his military intelligence activities in the war joined that view of the land with his passion for collecting period surveys and land transfer documents. He carried these interests well into his nineties until he died in 2004, and without those interests, what is resolved in this brief history would not have been possible.

Accompanying Morris were others of the same complexion, who also bridged the old Saugerties with what came after the war. Jean Wrolsen, in her newspaper column writings, and Harvey Fite, in his quarryman's museum at *Opus 40*, are two of the most influential. Together they form

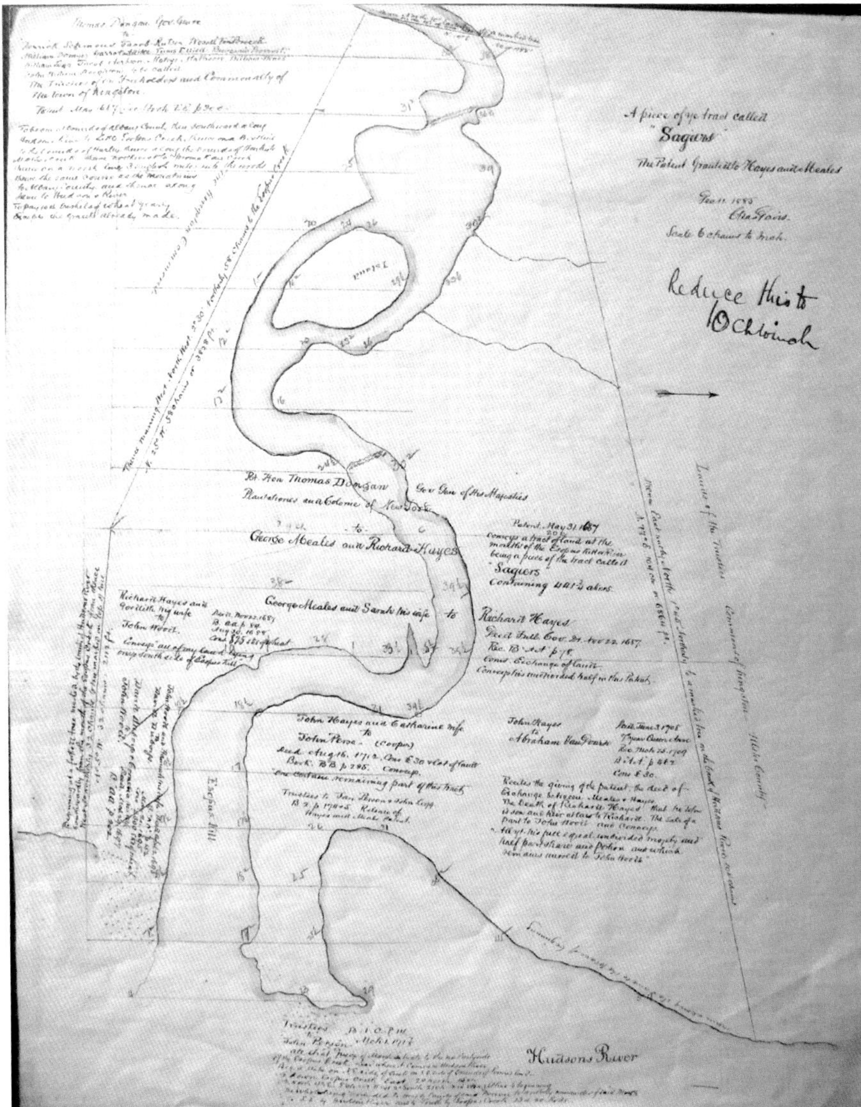

In the 1880s, Saugerties' origins in the Meales and Hayes Patent were explained through displays such as this by Judge Charles Davis. *R&L Archive collection.*

the pantheon of those who cross the mind of every thinking person with any level of real interest in Saugerties today. The ways they related their personal and professional interests to the historical context surrounding them—Fite in his sculpture, Wrolsen in her poetry and Rosenblum in his records and collecting—are of particular importance to history's relationship to a stabile Saugerties.

They—and in their time, surely others like them, coming from experiences in academia, the law and intelligence collection—would be expected to be inspired by the research, detective work and pure romance the understanding of history requires. But today there is a robust environment made to satisfy that passion that half a century ago could only have been dreamed of. Today uncovering historical facts no longer requires the specialized environments of their backgrounds but is available from nearly every popular Internet medium. Morris's interest would be exhausted by Virtual Earth. Jean's curiosity about the facts behind intimate tales would have her lost forever in online period newspaper archives. Harvey's insatiable curiosity about the elevation of work of hands to skill and art would be intrigued forever in the variety of interpretation found in every form on the Internet.

Despite all of today's resources, though, nothing can compete with the intellectual experience of the collections left from their years. This brief history is but an introduction to the local history room of the Saugerties Public Library dedicated to Jean Wrolson and to the massive archive of the Lamb Center housing the collections of Morris Rosenblum and, of course, the soul of Saugerties, Harvey Fite's *Opus 40* and that entire inspirational environment. They are what has created the common ground for a conversation on reaching a consensus on the single history that is written here.

Where there is a broad yearning for this consensus, history becomes a passion. And when everyone has equal access to that, this elevates a heritage destination to a pilgrimage site. When that level of history is known and shared it becomes a universal standard for an identity.

1

COLONIAL SAUGERTIES

Official records that prove a chain of title are steeped in history that is impossible to ignore. Records can never be dismissed. Ownership of land is not something that happens with a handshake or is passed on by hearsay. Land tenure is a tenuous thing if it's not sure, and there's no value in it unless it's clear.

In the Hudson Valley, recorded history starts with Henry Hudson having a meal with the chiefs of the Catskill and Esopus tribes on his *Half Moon* on September 26, 1609, while anchored at the border of their territories on the Hudson River at Saugerties. These chiefs gesture to the northwest and southwest past the corners of the point where the Catskill escarpment nearly touches the river. Hudson gives them gifts, and they share smoking tobacco. When this act is recorded by Robert Juet, Hudson's first mate, and his journal is published in Europe a dozen years later, there is an establishment date created for the history of Saugerties and maybe even a treaty and land transfer.

Records after this first event are made up of a Native American making a swap using an unknown language to name landmarks of a property a European believes he is buying. Those with the right to stake a claim based on these strange words written on paper and read back to a sachem who made his "mark" to attest to their correctness were those with the connections to the director or governor representing the king, queen or staats general or some other high official whose seal on a patent officially accepted those foreign words for whatever they believed them to mean.

History is written by the conquerors. The first generations of the earliest settlers, in the seventeenth century and into the next, were accustomed to strong autocratic rule. The Dutch directors, such as Peter Stuyvesant, were military men, as were the English governors beginning with Richard Nicolls and Edmond Andros. Church officials were selected based on the authority of the classis of Amsterdam for the Dutch and the king of England for the English. Generally speaking, the population accepted that their lives, including what they owned, were subject to that authoritarian control.

There is, however, a twist to our history. There's always a percentage of every group that has a greater need for independence and firmly stated legal rights that preserve it. Two concepts of this time in history helped. The Dutch had their Burgher Rights under their federal system, and the English had Rights of Englishmen under the Magna Carta.

On two occasions in the seventeenth century, a desire to exert these rights was attempted, counter to the general population's complacency. Both times they were initiated by the Dutch of New York.

The first was in the acceptance by Nicolls of the Dutch Freedoms and Exemptions rights of merchants and patroons to their property and inheritance customs in the surrender of Stuyvesant in 1664. Then in 1683, after the withholding of custom payments by the Dutch caused a financial crisis, they were allowed to elect representatives and meet in assembly. From that, a list of "rights and liberties" corresponding to the Rights of Englishmen was submitted and actually accepted by the proprietor, the Duke of York, in 1684.

This was subsequently disallowed by the Kings Council the following year once the duke became King James II. But that setback is what proved to be the deciding factor in the creation of Saugerties as an official place. It set the stage for the establishment of the Corporation of Kingston, the starting point for nearly every deed to the ownership of land in Saugerties.

The spirit of the earth is irrepressible. Water, rock and the natural product of the soil have dominion over history—over the presence of man. Nowhere is this statement more a brief history of man's temporal occupancy than where the Maniteau's Sopus reaches Mahicanituk, where the waters of the Catskill escarpment, the Wall of Maniteau, reach the Hudson River's arm of the sea: Saugerties.

The territory under the face of the Catskills was settled late and only when there was a need to tap its agricultural potential. Since its first settlement in 1651, this land, known at that time as the Esopus, went through two wars to take its fertile plantation lands from the native occupants. Title to

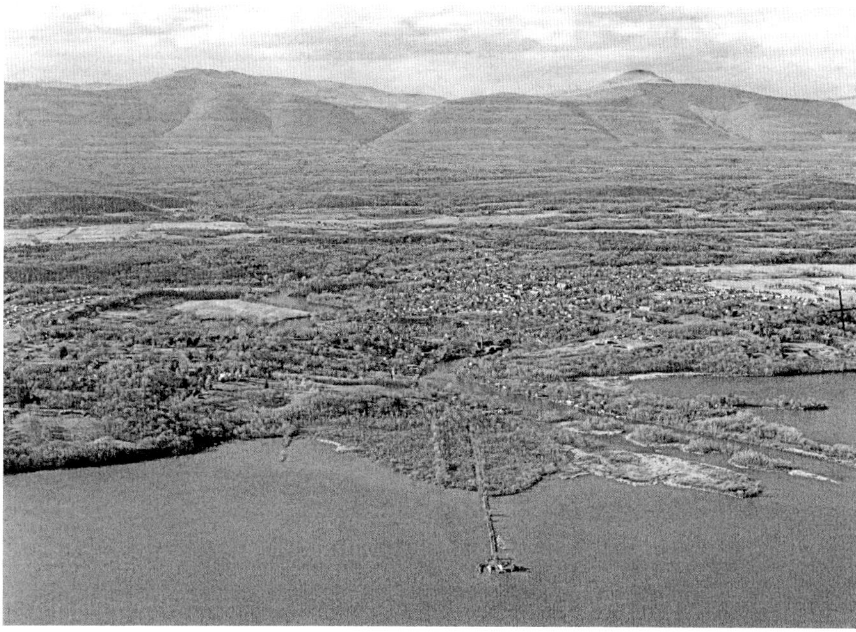

This view from over the Hudson presents the mountain and water resources that positioned Saugerties to play a part in American history. *R&L Archive collection.*

the land of Saugerties thus originated in conquest. From the time of these conquests, the settlement of the Esopus continually grew until it became the major supplier of grain, dairy and meat products to the English sugar plantations of the Caribbean, and that relationship to the economic stability of the time gave it power.

At the peak of its importance, in 1687, this Esopus territory was primarily under the control of the families of the original Dutch settlers who arrived in 1651. They had become influential enough to command two seats on the thirteen-member assembly that drafted the "rights and liberties" in 1683. In 1686, twelve of these Esopus Dutch were presenting a petition for a patent to lands that had been ceded by the natives in the Andros Treaty of 1677, land representing most of the area of the Esopus where Saugerties lies today. The land was north of their home village of Kingston in the territory called De Sagiers.

At face value, this was a petition not unlike the one granted to the south to twelve Huguenot partners ten years earlier for the land of New Paltz. They had purchased that land from the same natives who had relinquished it under this same treaty.

Colonel Thomas Dongan, governor at this time, had been dealing with numerous demands from the Dutch related to the 1664 treaty obligations. These demands conflicted with rights to assembly that England was not allowing to its colonial subjects. Whether by direct request from the Esopus petitioners or as a general appeasement gesture to the Dutch, Dongan chose to issue this patent together with, and inseparable from, corporate governance powers, all within the same document, as the Kingston Patent. In one sweeping measure, this document established an enclave of liberties for the Dutch they had nowhere else in New York.

The purpose may have been to focus their attention on a single gesture, but this proved to be revolutionary. Dongan had made the patent request from one covering just the northern treaty lands of De Sagiers to one covering all the territory then recognized as the Esopus. He made its area total about sixty-four thousand acres—one hundred square miles—running ten miles along the west shore of the Hudson River directly south from the line between the original Ulster and Albany Counties.

He then didn't grant the patent to the individual petitioners but to "one body corporate and politique to be called by the name of the Trustees of the Freeholders and Commonality of the Town of Kingston" and named the petitioners as this body's initial trustees. This town of Kingston would eventually encompass what are today the towns of Esopus, Ulster, Kingston and Saugerties and the city of Kingston, an area of nearly 140 square miles.

There are two key words relative to the way Dongan crafted this document that would eventually make this town into the Kingston Commons. These are *patent* and *corporate*. A patent in the seventeenth century was an official right to own land in exchange for an annual payment to the colonial proprietor or Crown. The patent is a deeded ownership to the soil, but the use of that land is governed by the jurisdiction it falls in and the ownership right must conform to that government's laws.

A corporation, on the other hand, is a chartered right from the Crown to govern as a municipal body through an elected instead of appointed governing body. It is a charter to make laws, hold court, tax a population and so forth. With the creation of a corporation with rights to the soil the colonial governor, with the seal of the Kings Council in 1688, was allowing something very unique for a colony: a patent to land owned and governed by the large group of citizens who already occupied it.

There were many patents owned by partners, such as the New Paltz patent jointly owned by twelve individuals. But they had no governance rights. This Kingston Patent was granted to a corporation made up of

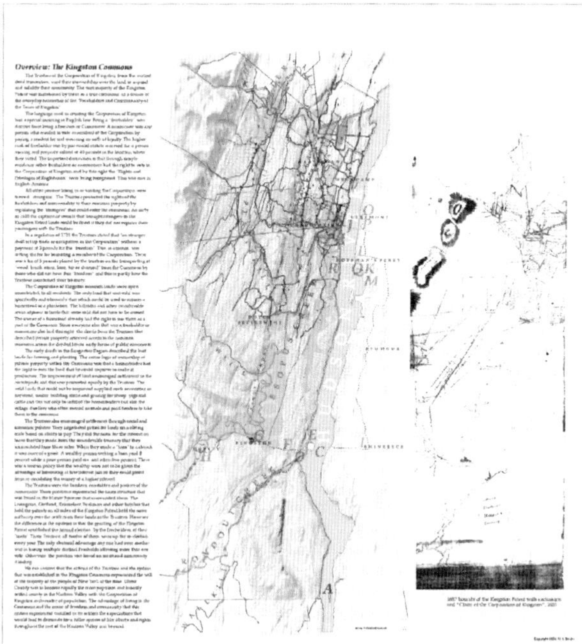

Left: The Saugerties of colonial times was within common lands on the frontier of the Corporation of Kingston. *From the author's History Atlas of Saugerties.*

Below: In the 1777 Revolutionary War burning of Kingston, Saugerties was the destination of the British fleet. *From the author's History Atlas of Saugerties.*

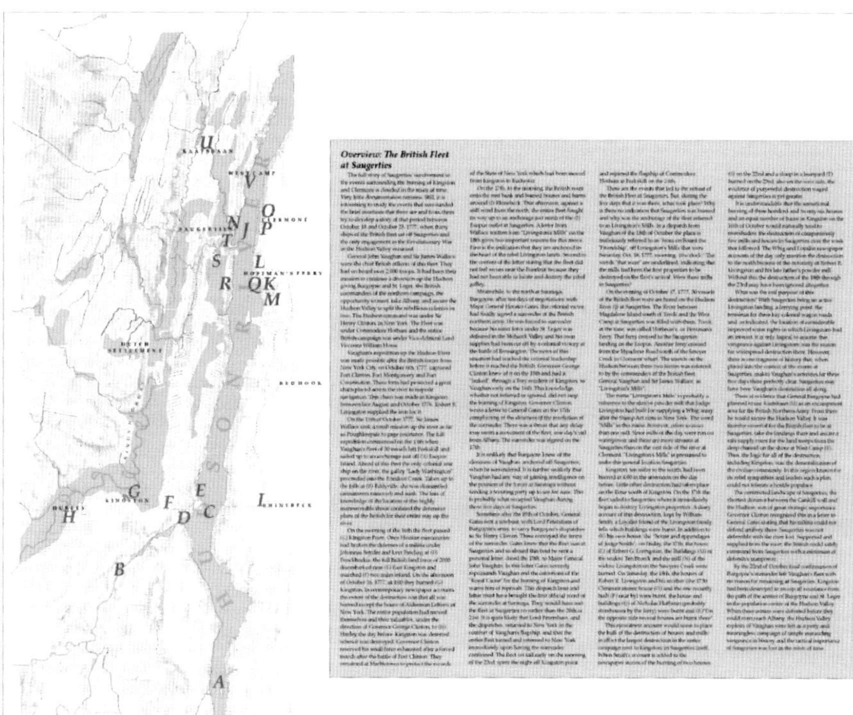

an unspecified commonality that could be changeable year to year but, nonetheless, had the right to elect each year a body of twelve from among them to govern their affairs.

This was indeed a unique institution in colonial America. If not the first, Kingston was among the first of a very small number of corporations created in the English colonies in all of their existence. By comparison, New York City was not granted a charter as a corporation until 1730, and even then its highest officials were appointed by the governor and they owned no land above high water. The Dutch Reformed Church of Kingston did not receive its corporate charter until 1710, and its consistory was still under a Dominie supervised from Holland.

With the creation of the Corporation of Kingston, the Esopus immediately became the focus of Dutch culture and a magnet for Dutch interests in New York. The rights to assemble and elect representatives and be governed by peers were chartered rights there, and the ownership of property and the right to establishment of a business were all locally granted rights. Quickly, investment in village property and the building of Dutch-friendly business environments boomed. Thus began a path to what ninety years later would be recognized as a home to such a radical population that the total destruction of Kingston could be justified during the Revolution—the only such incident during the entire war.

The targeting of Kingston for destruction in 1777 was due to a combination of highly symbolic factors. The town of Kingston occupied a critical geographic position relative to commerce. It is where a centralized land route, the King's Highway, links the southern colonies to the Hudson River. To be represented as a merchant of Kingston was to be in a position to support inter-colony commerce, and this became a decisively important position to be in as these colonies moved closer to rebellion.

The liberties long enjoyed in Kingston since 1687 became symbolic of the rights that were sought in a new national identity in 1776. So when the citizens of Kingston published and read on its courthouse steps the first constitution of the new state of New York in April 1777, it did not go unnoticed that this had been drafted in the same place their trustees met after their annual election one month earlier. Seven months later, the British fleet would burn this courthouse, this meeting room and all other houses, barns and places of commerce and places of worship in the entire village of Kingston.

But Kingston was more than a population center. It is called the Kingston Commons because, since its inception, the vast majority of its patent grant was used communally for grazing cattle, growing crops, quarrying stone and harvesting timber for lumber and firewood. In the commons, there were many dwelling houses along well-traveled wagon roads. Few, though, were on private land. There were also storage buildings and lower-level shelters for animals and field dwellings for slave laborers. There were sawmills and similar light industrial buildings. Much of this infrastructure had been placed there and communally maintained for going on a century. This was all well known to the working population of Kingston. Their homes were burned in the fall, and it was in the commons that they spent their winter, the same winter so memorialized by the hardships of Valley Forge.

At the end of the Revolutionary War, when it was time to join New York to a nation under a national constitution, Kingston was again looked to for its century of experience in self-governance. Indeed, the strength of this symbolism even assumed for a short period that the capital of this new nation would be on the Hudson's shores in Kingston Commons' Flatbush on the present Saugerties southern border. That was not to be, but what this symbolism did accomplish was an even greater tribute to this powerful spirit. When New York held out for the promise of a bill of rights in exchange for its ratification of the Constitution, it was the voices of nearly five generations of the "freeholders and commonality" of Kingston that were heard as their place as the nation's capital was bartered away for a bill of rights.

Throughout the period up to the Revolution and after the rebuilding of Kingston, the Dutch made up the majority population within the Corporation of Kingston. They stubbornly resisted use of any language other than Dutch and continued in this well after Dutch ceased even to be the language of preaching in the center of their culture, the Dutch Reformed Church. As a people and society, this only served to emphasize their minority status in the overall English-speaking population of the new state and nation. As a consequence, the Kingston Commons was a pariah in post-Revolution New York once its status was no longer politically unique. When the Corporation of Kingston's municipal authority was given over to a state-sanctioned township to be divided into standard-sized towns, the trustees no longer had any function except as what would be termed today a condominium board. They thus decided in 1803 to survey the commons into lots, sell them to the population and disband.

The trustees' plan for the sale of these lots would prove to have a lasting effect on the social makeup of the towns its lots occupied. That plan sold the lots based on a graduated pricing, depending on the length of residency of the purchaser in the Corporation of Kingston. Also the prime lots and lots of

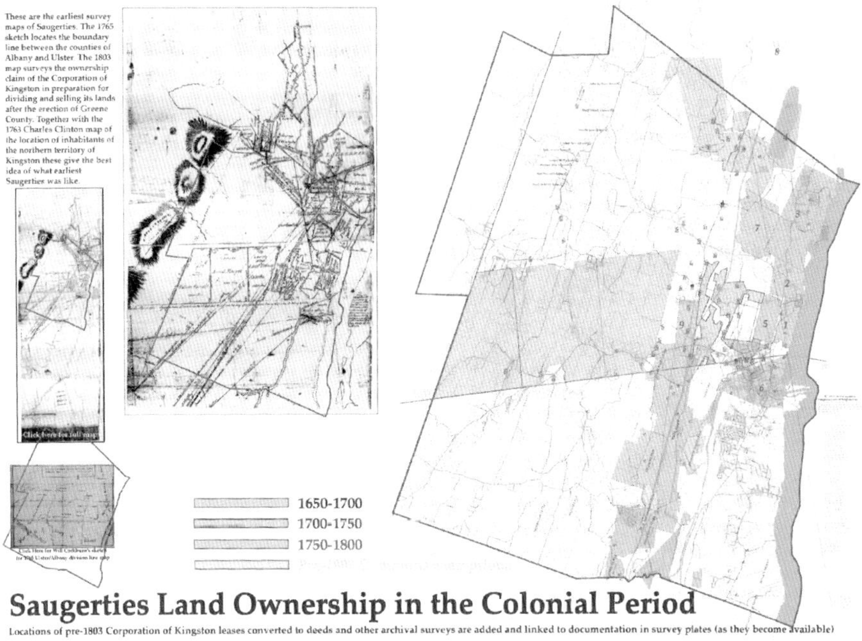

Deeded ownership of land in Saugerties was not common before the division of Kingston's Commons in 1803. *From the author's History Atlas of Saugerties.*

larger size were first offered to those of the longest residency. The larger lots went to heads of households born in and residing in the commons possessing a freehold valued at over £200. Heirs to someone born in the commons and themselves residing in the commons fitting the same financial criteria were also entitled to these larger lots. Those meeting the same criteria of residency but possessing a less valuable freehold, not less than £100, were entitled to the smaller lots.

After these came those not born in the commons but residing there prior to 1777. They were also entitled to the smaller lots if they had a freehold of over £100, but they paid more. Last in line were those who fit the same financial criteria but had taken up settlement after 1777. They were entitled to the same size small lots but paid even more.

There was a hidden purpose in this plan. The financial criteria they used for purchase qualification related also to voting requirements, and this related to the political influence of Kingston in elections for state and national representatives. This was to be degraded with the division of Kingston into smaller towns. So by their division method and selling criteria, the trustees were allowing a Dutch electorate to select which town they would place their future and the future of their families' political influence in. A critical mass of any one influential group would be able to structure the bounds of any one of the three new townships that were to be formed out of the ancient Corporation of Kingston town.

So the political clout of this landed Dutch relic of colonial New York would go on ruling the government and commerce around Kingston until a decisive battle with progressive interests finally dissolved its base and the city of Kingston and the town of Ulster were carved out of Kingston in 1875. In this part of the late nineteenth century, at about the same time the Pilgrim fathers were becoming more fashionable as a symbol of America's founding principles, necessitating the burial of our Dutch legacy to achieve that purpose, the Kingston Commons also fell victim to the editor of time and the schoolbook and thus vanished from memory. Eventually, nothing remained of this once great institution but the occasional reference in surveys and deeds to the classes and lots it sold between 1803 and when it ceased to exist legally in 1816.

2

BIRTH OF THE TOWN OF SAUGERTIES

On April 5, 1811, the Town of Saugerties was incorporated, and the first business of its new governing body was to survey the Woodstock road from the river to "where the aforesaid road intersects the Ulster and Delaware first branch turnpike-road." The concern this survey embodied would define the growth of Saugerties' political boundaries, its influence as a major industrial and mercantile center and its identity as a separate community from Kingston for the rest of its existence.

The new town was all private property when it formed, and roads had been standardized in deeds by the trustees of the Corporation of Kingston to adhere to customs followed in Kingston Commons for over a century. Most of the new Saugerties private ownership had previously worked under the understanding that trespass was not limited and followed this custom of allowing any freeholder the right of passage.

The development potential of east–west roads as turnpikes was this new government's concern. Turnpikes attracted the interest of speculators. In 1804, the Ulster and Delaware Turnpike had climbed over the Catskill Mountains, and the state legislature had approved the establishment of a corporation to build an extension from its end on the Susquehanna 160 additional miles into the interior of the state. By 1811, the resulting traffic heading for Saugerties as a destination was a major concern of the town whose borders covered a span from two thousand feet up in the Catskills down to the tidewater of the Hudson River.

Many names like Snyder, Trumpbour, Wynkoop, Post, Brink, Wolven, Miller, Myer, Mynderse, Marterstock, Oosterhout, Overbaugh, Freleigh, Hummell, Diedrich, Schoonmaker and Kiersted had owned and worked the land of this part of Kingston for generations before its soil became Saugerties. A tradition of maintaining the land as open, large estate farms in the late nineteenth and early twentieth centuries involved re-consolidations of those original Dutch and German Palatine family farms, so some evidence of them appears right up to the present day.

Virtually every deed to the lands of the Kingston Commons in Saugerties has a property line bordering or crossing one of the many extinct roads that once were daily traveled between the hamlets and these farms. Remnants of these roads, when found on a wooded lot along overgrown stone walls, are a reminder of the time when generation after generation harmoniously passed freely from one part of the land to the other.

Private ownership of lands that had been commonly used for generations was an issue. Lands in the Saugerties region had been used for grazing. With ordinances passed down from the state and overseen by fence wardens stipulating that fences be laid to keep animals from straying, the new town was already being crisscrossed by stone walls, forming a constant reminder of the Kingston Commons division map's grid of straight lines perpendicular to and parallel to the wall of the Catskill escarpment.

The rights to the area that had just become the town of Saugerties had been unsettled for decades in an ancient dispute over the exact division between the original Ulster and Albany Counties. The very people who now were citizens of Saugerties had been the subject of Kingston's claims in colonial times as their homesteads formed the defensive buffer that protected its common lands and that it recognized as part of its militia in both the French and Indian War and the Revolutionary War. These Palatine settlers had experienced a century of insecurity, and they naturally turned to protecting the routes between themselves from the interference of outsiders this new freedom to sell land made a possibility.

This preoccupation with any restriction to land access began when the three towns formed in 1811 out of the Kingston Patent's colonial township had their boundaries follow lots that had been sold after an 1803 survey of Kingston's common lands. The agrarian population of the new town of Saugerties was the most affected by this change in status.

That survey of 1803 was in two phases. The first mapped all the documented claims of the Corporation of Kingston to firm up the exact bounds of the town of Kingston. This survey was to place the northern

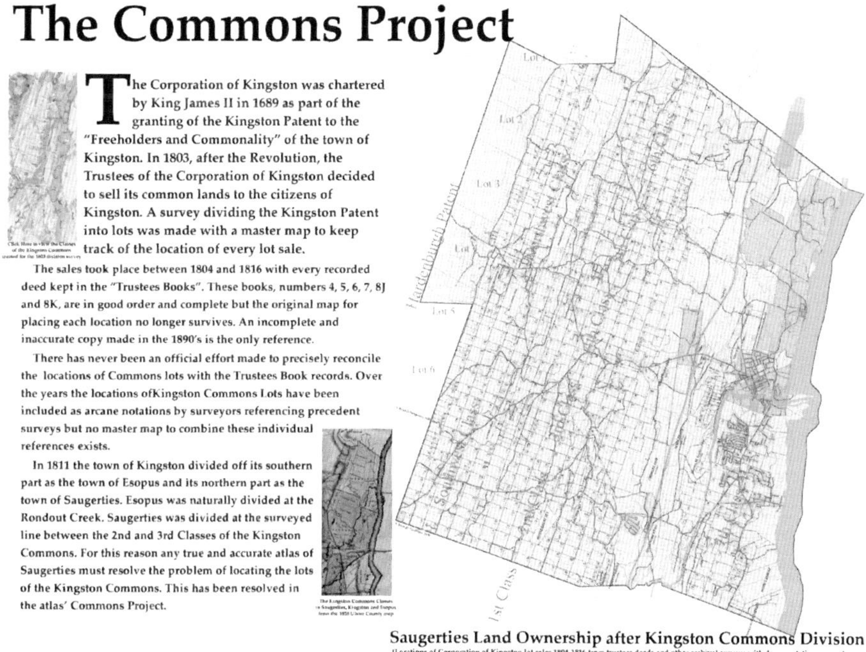

The Commons Project

The Corporation of Kingston was chartered by King James II in 1689 as part of the granting of the Kingston Patent to the "Freeholders and Commonality" of the town of Kingston. In 1803, after the Revolution, the Trustees of the Corporation of Kingston decided to sell its common lands to the citizens of Kingston. A survey dividing the Kingston Patent into lots was made with a master map to keep track of the location of every lot sale.

The sales took place between 1804 and 1816 with every recorded deed kept in the "Trustees Books". These books, numbers 4, 5, 6, 7, 8J and 8K, are in good order and complete but the original map for placing each location no longer survives. An incomplete and inaccurate copy made in the 1890's is the only reference.

There has never been an official effort made to precisely reconcile the locations of Commons lots with the Trustees Book records. Over the years the locations ofKingston Commons Lots have been included as arcane notations by surveyors referencing precedent surveys but no master map to combine these individual references exists.

In 1811 the town of Kingston divided off its southern part as the town of Esopus and its northern part as the town of Saugerties. Esopus was naturally divided at the Rondout Creek. Saugerties was divided at the surveyed line between the 2nd and 3rd Classes of the Kingston Commons. For this reason any true and accurate atlas of Saugerties must resolve the problem of locating the lots of the Kingston Commons. This has been resolved in the atlas' Commons Project.

The designation of Kingston Commons lots in the town of Saugerties is the origin of most land ownership. *From the author's History Atlas of Saugerties.*

border that had extended into what was then Albany County. Most of that is in what is today Saugerties.

When a border was settled on, this line became the boundary between the towns of Kingston and Catskill and also the line dividing the new Greene County from an extended Ulster County. All of this newly defined town of Kingston up to the new Greene County border was "the claim of the Corporation of Kingston."

The second phase of the 1803 survey divided this total claim into rectangles of mostly thirty- and forty-five-acre lots, with these lots made manageable by numbering them in large divisions called classes.

A half dozen of these classes were south of the Rondout Creek in the present town of Esopus. They were, by name, the South of Rondout Second Class East of Road, the South of Rondout Second Class South of Road, South of Rondout First Class, the Huzzy Hill lots, the Shappawanick Mountain lots and Kline Esopus lots.

Nine of the classes were around the present-day city of Kingston and, by 1875, in the town of Ulster and a much-diminished town of Kingston.

These were, by name, the Binnewater Class, the Pine Bush Class, the Flat Bush Class, the Clove Class, the Three Mile Class, Compensation Class East of Road, Compensation Class West of Road and the Suppies Hook lots. Parts of the Southwest and all of the First and Second Class were also in 1811 in the town of Kingston.

The rest were in the town of Saugerties. Of present-day Saugerties, 80 percent is on the footprint of part or all of eleven Kingston Commons classes. These are, by name, most of the Southwest Class and, after 1832, the northernmost line of lots in the First Class and all of the Second, as well as all of the Third, Fourth, Fifth, Sixth, Northwest, Seventh, Plantasie Bergh and the West of the Esopus Kill lots that have been part of Saugerties since it became a town in 1811.

The occupied farms leased previous to the survey as homesteads of the original settlers of Saugerties are deeded at this time with their descriptions marked within and adjacent to lot bounds where numbered lot corners or lines are used as references for their locations. Together, these and the grid divisions describe nearly all the land westward from the hills that are west

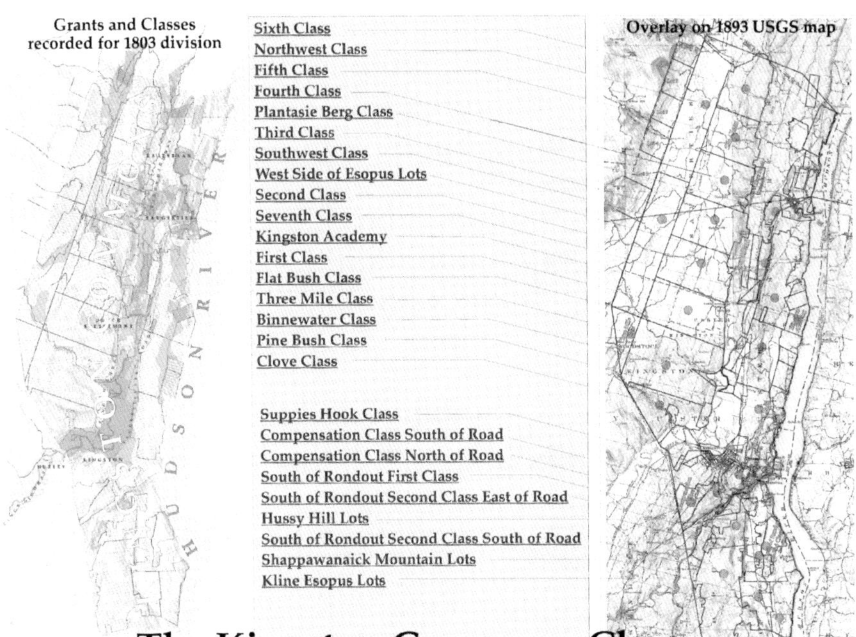

Classes and individual lots of the 1803 division of the Corporation of Kingston became boundaries for the towns. *From the author's History Atlas of Saugerties.*

of the Thruway and south of the village from the hills that are east of the Thruway on to the river.

In excess of 650 individual deeds to just the lots that are in Saugerties are recorded in what are called the Trustees Books, numbered 1 through 8. The latter four of these books are made up of printed boilerplate deeds with handwritten date, purchaser's and trustee's names, lot description and reservation of trespass rights to common access. All of books 5 and 6 and most of 7 are deeds recorded in 1804, with books 1, 2, 3, 4 and the rest of 7 and the J, K and L parts of book 8 recording deeds that range in time from 1687 to the last sale from the trustees in 1816.

The Kingston Commons

Ownership of land in Saugerties has always been a relative concept. Lands tended to blend one into another. By law, rights of trespass were included in deeds from the Corporation of Kingston, and up to the latter decades of the nineteenth century, seasonal demands of farming and the fact that most of the rural community was related by marriage made the working of the land of Saugerties for over two centuries a communal activity. Wynkoop-Myer-Schoonmaker and Trumpbour-Cockburn-Fiero family co-ops were unofficial but recognizable to each other in their techniques of keeping their land. Deeds of parcels often bounced back and forth between these family groupings based on financial necessities or gifting between generations.

A tradition of sharing out land, or land leases, that dated back to the Corporation of Kingston, was maintained as a method of admitting new farming members into the community, particularly as the demands of working the large farms stressed the capacity of the older families. But the ownership generally remained intact, continuing the constant accessibility to lands for generations well into the mid-twentieth century.

This is what muddies what began as an exact science. The original surveys of 1803 are missing, and a map made in the 1890s by Edward Codwise that is much referenced but missing parts and very schematic in form has names applied to lots that have been found to reflect the supposed ownership in Codwise's time. Surveyors like Codwise have continually tried to reconstruct the 1803 surveys as an aid for title searches, but extensive research to locate exact positions of lot corners relative to a large collection of period surveys is only a recent subject of interest.

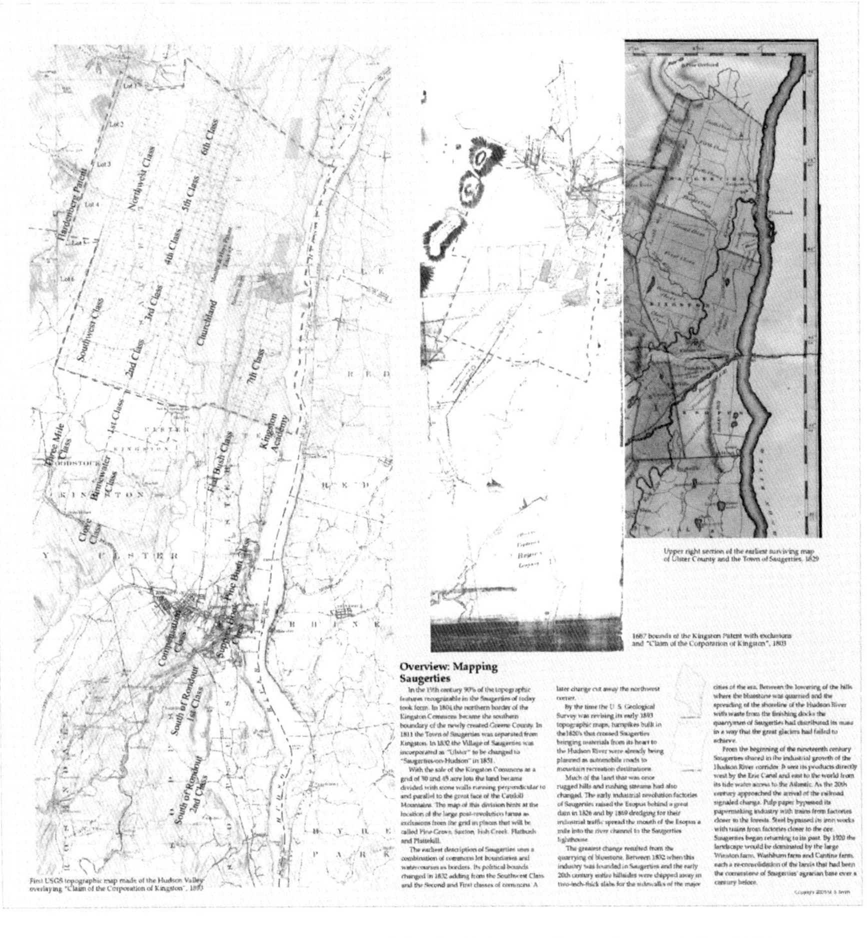

The commons lot locations used in the original 1811 town formation and the 1832 annexation are precisely placed. *From the author's History Atlas of Saugerties.*

The events and personages of Saugerties history act on a stage that is defined by the history of the land. They may be facts frozen in records, but the actual locations of their performance is what is important to history. The best way to place these in time is to create that place on a map of the Kingston Commons at the time the town begins.

Building an accurate map of the original surveys is not a completely onerous task. Every deed is a building block rectangle on a linear grid with each referencing corners of others in its description. Nearly all descriptions use right angle directions of 66° SE or NW and 24° NE or SW. All the deed descriptions are written in measurements of chains and links to confirm the lot area. Every lot also has an original owner.

A reference to the commons is in the formation record for the town of Saugerties, and this provides the key to the precise locating of every commons lot created in 1803. This 1811 document names a lot by class and number, applies sixty-six- and twenty-four-degree angles to it and uses chains as a measure in the town's boundary dimension translatable to a scale for every commons lot.

The town's west-to-south corner gives both the key angle and position of lot number 17 in the Southwest Class as its starting point. A precise scale for this lot is made possible when the length of the sides of this key angle and the set landmark of the Plattekill Creek as an endpoint are given. From there, it is possible to correctly proportion and position all the rest of the lot rectangles to the overall map since all their deeds use adjacent lots in their descriptions. Even the odd lot description with non-rectangular measurements can be drafted to fill a void by applying this 1803 base angle to plot its shape.

This Saugerties corner reference applies to the entire Kingston Patent because the lots continue into bordering towns. Once this map that verifies the proportions of the individual commons lots is made, then it is reasonably logical that a similar matching process for locating the rest of the commons lots in the classes of the towns to the south would be accurate.

However, aligning present property boundaries to these commons lots has proven to be somewhat a challenge. Matches to topographical features such as stream banks and roadsides in property descriptions and property surveys show inaccuracies compared to their originating lot positions.

So it appears that at a certain point in history the commons deeds were ignored, and so the survey that is the historical origin of land ownership in Saugerties has a hard time reconciling with the current property divisions of the tax map that is based on twentieth-century surveys.

The concept of the Kingston Commons division is a template that demands any present-day property's location be dead-on accurate. To surveyors, this is the ultimate benefit of mapping the commons. But for the history of Saugerties, there are other benefits of knowing about the commons that are not as officious as locating dead-on property lines. Land in Saugerties is central to nineteenth-century events, be it resources or railroads, and the Kingston Commons and lots in classes find themselves connected to some curious details in the town's history.

Period events and the references of diaries use words and names that trustees' deeds use as place names or names of those owning adjacent property. Some names included on early survey drawings are also archaic, with no current reference, but all the same must be understood.

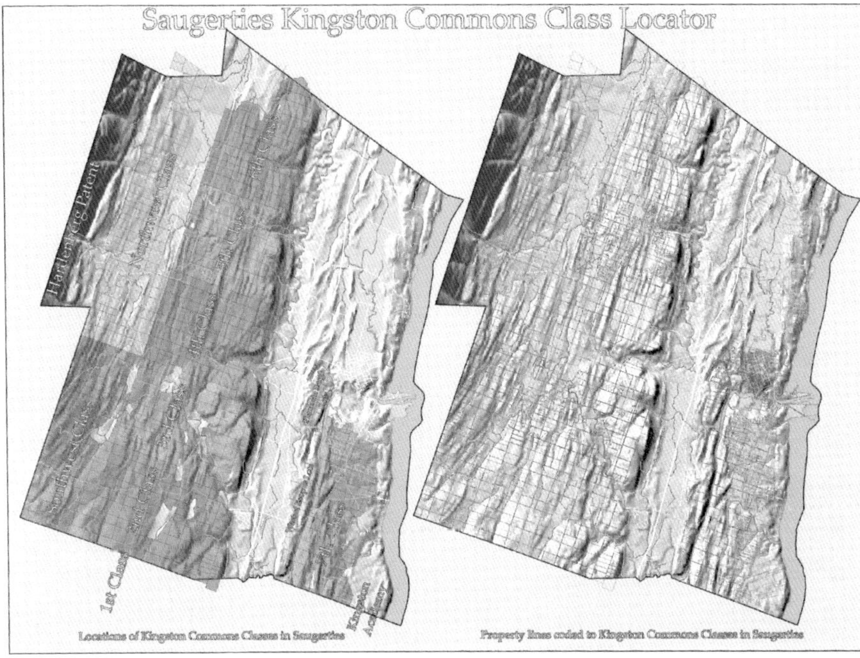

The terrain of Saugerties played an important part in the position of commons lots and current property lines. *From the author's History Atlas of Saugerties.*

A quick look at a real estate or tax lien notice in a late nineteenth-century newspaper shows that both the commons lot and class and the bounds ownership methods were used to describe and locate a property. Except in the case of the rare traditionalist surveyor's knowledge, these references are totally obscure today. The language in ancient deeds and leases that offers so many insights into the composition of the community of the day and how its economy worked is unavailable to history without the Kingston Commons deeds and their locations' use as a Rosetta stone.

The fact that Kingston Commons lots were sold based on a graduated scale depending on the length of residency in the Corporation of Kingston is of great historical value. There is a genealogical importance to these lot sales because they can be traced to individuals and their post- and pre-Revolution residency and personal worth, adding a method for tracing lineage into this early period for individuals who may not have fallen into the normal church records. This resolves most former speculation on settlement patterns in the early eighteenth century in Saugerties. Even basic variations of spelling of the same familiar word, written as heard from a Dutch speaker as opposed to a decidedly English surname, give a clue to the genesis of the current words in use today.

The markers that are all around Saugerties for what are presumed to be historic sites were first placed 80 years ago. At that time, their information was from 30 years before and was written about events that happened 120 years before it. The treasure trove of place names and descriptions of physical and historical features that work their way into the descriptions written into the originating Kingston Commons deeds helps resolve much of the lore these markers represent.

The fact that so many of these descriptions were written in the short period of five weeks between January and March 1804 implies that many inhabitants concurred on place names. For instance, when present-day Wilhelm Road is consistently described as Blue Mountain Road in every deed that uses it as a boundary, that is not only what everyone called it in 1804, but it also indicates that it was the main road used to get to Blue Mountain for those who traveled from there down to the river. And when a schoolhouse and spring are excluded from a deed that is simply described as "under the blue mountain" and adjoining both the Fourth and Fifth classes, the place on the map where this is cannot be where the old Blue Mountain schoolhouse of today is. Logically then, there is some reason to conjecture that Wilhelm Road to High Falls Road to Fawn Road and on past this schoolhouse location over present-day Blue Mountain Road through VanBuskirk, Band Camp and Pine Lane was a thoroughfare in 1804 and may have been the route taken in the story of a Woodstock family returning from church at Kaatsbaan during the Revolutionary War.

Being able to go to a book and associate the earliest written account of land features and even houses, schools and mills with an actual location on a map is an obvious advantage of having the commons deeds as the basic reference for history. But aside from the discovery of names and features, awareness that the commons existed sheds light on the sense that there has been a movement of property lines throughout history. When tax maps were first made available in 1978, there were plenty of holes left between surveyed properties. Long before this town-wide reference, the lore among professionals was that surveying from the south needed different points of origin than from the north and the same east from west. The resultant overlaps and gaps were often resolved at a convenient middle ground, even by creating a diagonal split as a compromise.

If a grid based on the ancient lines of the commons division was available to those generating the first tax maps, they would have been

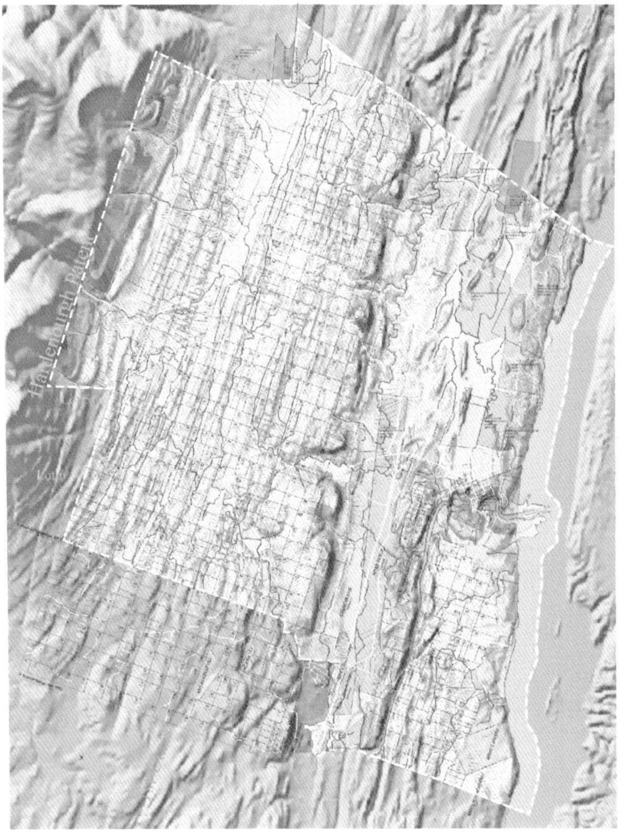

The town of Saugerties, formed in 1811, created a wedge between the Catskills and the Hudson on New York's map. *Interpretive map by the author.*

more accurate, and there would be more stable ground for surveyors. It is amazing that the obvious accuracy clearly available in the concept of the Kingston Commons division scheme of 1803 was not used as the root for every subsequent transfer after 1816. Since Saugerties is one of the few places in the region where this can be done, bragging rights about the preciseness of the division of its land should be as much a part of its heritage as any other part of its history.

3

THE COUNTRYSIDE

The two main industries of 1830s Saugerties—making purified iron and machine-made paper—both anticipated economic developments and product needs of future decades. Iron making would explode in demand with the coming of the railroads. The economy that the Erie Canal and westward expansion sparked stressed the supply of paper required by the increase in information and transactions.

It is not just innovativeness in the application of water power that Saugerties is a showcase for, but also the concept of being ahead of the demand curve. It was also way ahead of the curve in the social changes that were taking place in the Hudson Valley.

Both the Erie and the D&H Canals provided a focus on the Hudson River that would see the population of New York City balloon by the end of the 1820 decade. Within a year after the opening of the Erie Canal, forty barges a day would carry thousands of passengers and tens of thousands of bushels of grain per year from western New York and Ohio farms to the Port of New York, past Saugerties.

The farms of the Hudson Valley and especially the large tenant farmlands of the Livingstons had long profited from providing the flour, meat and firewood that sustained New York City's population. By the close of the 1820s, competitive prices bypassed them for this market. The growing grain belt of the Midwest and its meatpacking houses were supplying an endless flow of products along the Erie Canal, and D&H Canal coal was revolutionizing heating and cooking in the city.

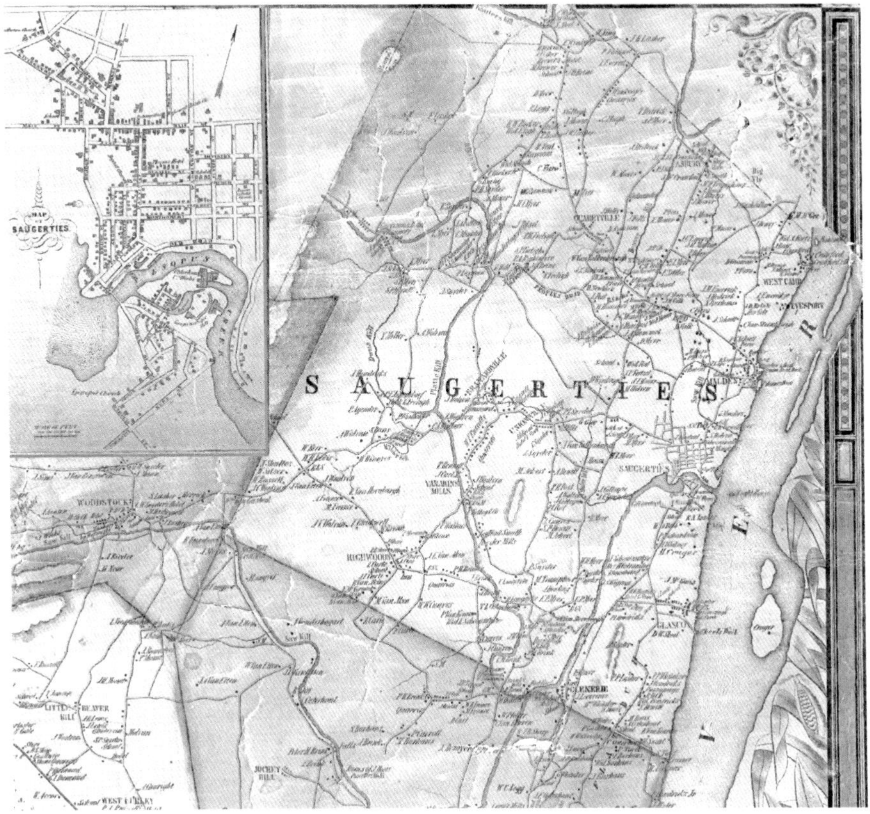

A composite of Saugerties represented on the 1853 Tillson and Brink wall map of Ulster County displays how prominent the town had become. *R&L Archive collection.*

The change brought about by the canal boom was nowhere more apparent than at Glasco. It brought an end to the great activity there that, for a short time, made it a major port on the Hudson. For a decade, cargoes that came down the Ulster and Delaware turnpike road by team lined the long parallel streets on its heights awaiting the sloops that would take them down to the New York markets. The great bay between Glasco and Tivoli allowed for a high level of river traffic in the day of sail, and Glasco was primed to have the commercial advantage of the best land and water assets. The U&D was for this period the shortest link between the wheat belt of central New York and the Hudson, and since the Esopus had always been the center of wheat trade, Glasco was a center of wheat deals and its transport.

Now, with shipping dropped from $100 a ton on the turnpike to under $9 on the canal, hundreds of teamsters, carters and market sloop captains, professions dominated by the Dutch since early colonial days, were put out of work. With the loss of the wheat trade, Glasco declined right along with the prestige and fortunes that both the old Esopus and the Manor families enjoyed from their long hold on the agrarian economy of the Hudson Valley. With this decline, the legendary power center of Esopus and its Kingston Commons fell into obscurity, to be nearly erased from memory within a generation.

A new standard of wealth was to take hold on the west bank of the Hudson. This new wealth was still based on the land, but on land that had been of no special importance to these early agrarian families. It was from what they regarded as worthless barrier palisades in South Kingston that a cement industry would grow. It was from the impassible high woods ledges and other unfertile land found so annoyingly useless in the Kingston Commons that would blossom a bluestone industry. And from the bluffs along the river where the soil clung to their plows like lard would grow the brick industry.

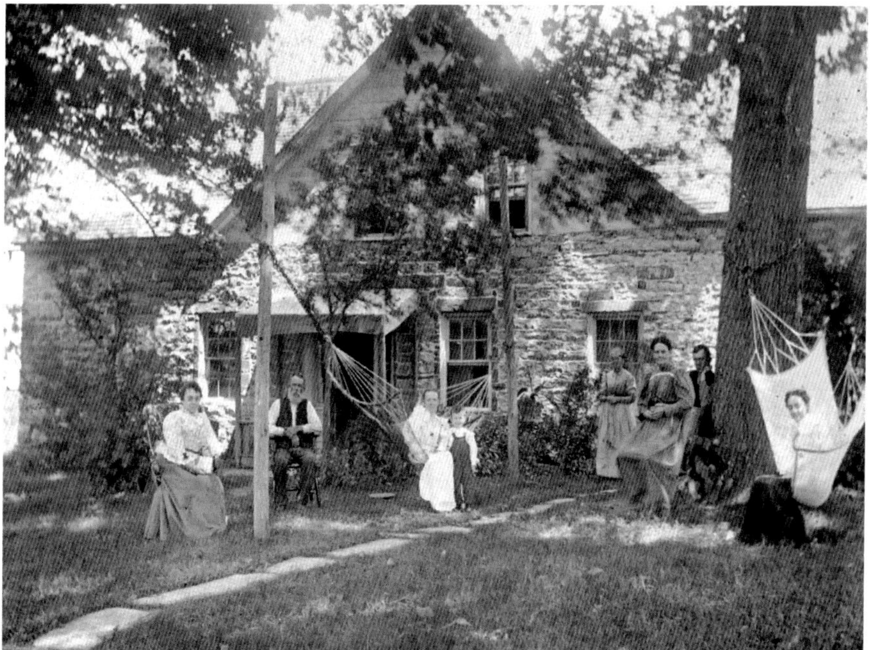

An earlier Myer stone house in the Churchland had a farm family that prospered from the village as their farm's main market. *From Jeanne Goldberg.*

This brought an enormous shift in the basic levels of society. The planting and herding activities that had long been carried out by the slaves of the large landholders or the tenants of the large manors as obligations were replaced by wage earning. With the gradual emancipation of slaves enacted in 1799 finally removing all slavery in the state by 1827, and other changes in the state constitution in 1847 recognizing life tenancies in the manors as deeds in actuality, the basic systems of labor that made large land holdings profitable suddenly required capital outlay to function. With the resultant breakup of the agrarian dynasties over the mid-decades of the nineteenth century, the Hudson Valley looked toward other ways to grow its economy.

The rivals for centers of the new economy of the old Esopus and Catskill Mountain regions were the ports of Rondout with the D&H Canal terminals and the quarrying of the Vlightberg for its limestone to make cement and the ports of Saugerties with the town's iron and papermaking industries and the quarrying of its bluestone ledges for the sidewalk slabs of the growing metropolises of the Atlantic coast.

The workers that this new economy attracted to Rondout and Saugerties were the Irish. During the short period between the founding of the town of Saugerties and the establishing of the villages of Rondout and Saugerties, the freed slaves of the early Dutch families nearly all left to live in New York City, and the influx of Irish immigrants into the city came upriver to fill the new limestone and bluestone quarrying jobs here. Like the workers they replaced, these new residents owned no land. But there were other Irish immigrants who came before them to work on the Erie and D&H Canals, as well as those brought in for the new industries of Saugerties. An Irish culture was present to welcome these new immigrants in the late 1830s. They were helped to settle and find access to ownership of the small farmland plots being parceled off by the earlier Dutch and Palatine landholders.

In the 1840s, the demand for bluestone was growing. Scores of shanty towns sprang up as quarrying spread to every outcrop between Russell's Clove in Saugerties and the heights of Mead Mountain in Woodstock. Nearly every one of these quarry sites was purchased through loans from Jeremiah Russell, every slab of bluestone quarried from these lands went to market by way of Jeremiah Russell's Saugerties and Woodstock Turnpike and nearly every cent paid for the slab at a Russell yard at the dock was spent at a Russell store.

By the 1840s, the Russell family was establishing its fourth generation of influence in the Saugerties community. The founder, John Ludwig Roesle, arrived before the Revolution and married into the fourth-generation

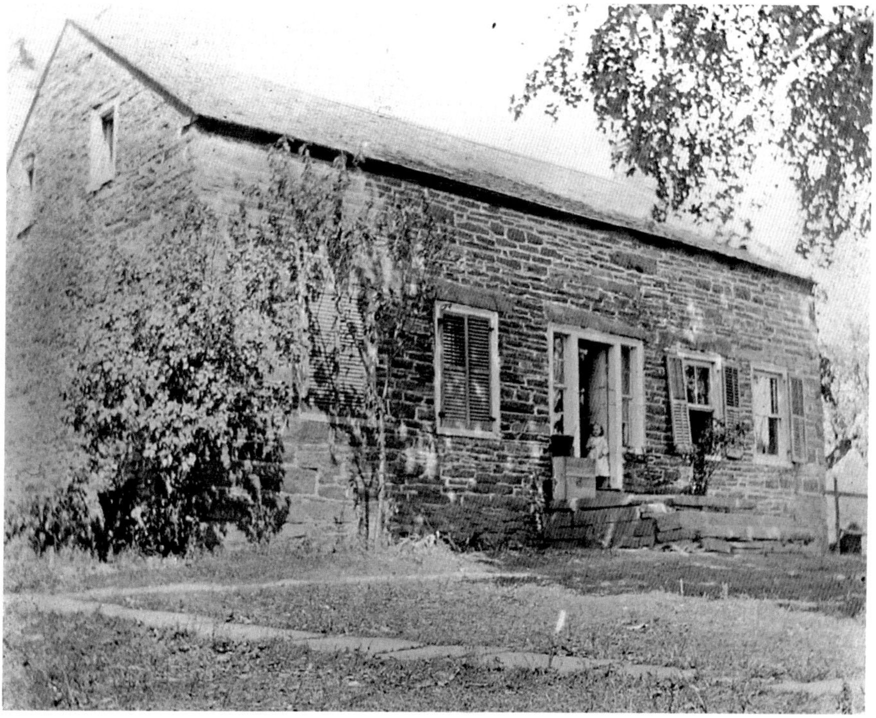

An earlier Pine Grove farm by 1900 had a family that worked the bluestone quarries along the Saugerties and Woodstock Turnpike. *From Jeanne Goldberg.*

Palatine Fiero family. By 1833, Jeremiah, his youngest son, had amassed a fortune as a merchant and was already passing this activity on to William F., a third-generation Russell, then only twenty-one.

From 1828 forward, Jeremiah Russell engaged himself increasingly in the field of finance and related commercial development. This was a time known for politicization of banking, and one of the reasons Saugerties was able to grow independently was because of the private banking services that Jeremiah Russell provided. His speculative insights on the value of land accessed by the Saugerties and Woodstock Turnpike caused him to be the largest holder of mortgage debt in the town.

Over a period of three decades, the growth of the town can be traced in the hundreds of deeds through which Jeremiah Russell moved subsistence farm families into hamlet and village residences opening their lands to quarrying, reselling their land to new families engaged in this livelihood. As this happened, hamlets grew, becoming a focus of small blacksmith, wheelwright and carpentry businesses built on the skills of the earlier farmers as they were directed toward new livelihoods supplying services to those working the quarries. Jeremiah Russell's profits from his land ventures were used to support their banking needs and also those of the larger industries and businesses of Saugerties Village. By the end of the nineteenth century, nearly three generations of Saugerties' inhabitants had lived knowing no other system than this locally interactive economy.

The tides of social change that accompanied the industrialization period of the 1830s and '40s profoundly affected the native culture of Saugerties. Up until this time, the predominant language was Dutch. It was the language of the farmworker, the teamster, the boatman. When the many slaves of the mid-Hudson Dutch were freed in 1827, they went to New York City, mainly because they knew only Dutch, and that was still the language of the carters, dock workers and boatmen there. With the importation of workers for the mills and the opening of the quarries, the predominant language of Saugerties had become, almost overnight, English.

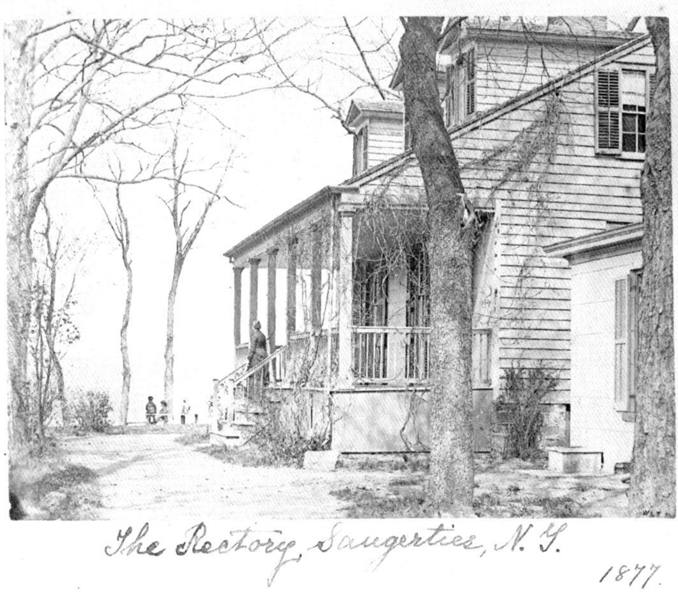

New dwellings on village streets followed the styles and materials of countryside houses, while farms still dominated its surroundings. *From Audrey Klinkenberg.*

Native Dutch-speaking Jeremiah Russell had an English-speaking wife. By 1833, he had transferred all his merchant activities to his son, William F., whose wife and brother-in-law partner hailed from Connecticut. Their newly re-formed merchant business engaged in the sale of bluestone to the docks of Manhattan on sloops captained by the Dutch families of Saugerties. By the 1850s, the fourth generation, the grandchildren of Jeremiah Russell, were marrying into the oldest Dutch families of the town, the Russell wealth helping to reestablish the influence of the threatened Dutch culture. In 1855, the name of the village of Ulster was changed to Saugerties as an expression of a desire to preserve this association with a pre-industrial Dutch heritage. In the 1880 *History of Ulster County*, a grandchild of Jeremiah Russell, Frederick T. Russell, is heralded as the current exponent of Dutch culture, having married Julia R. Mynderse and occupying her ancestral John Persen 1712 stone house on the river in the village of Saugerties.

The influence of the landed Dutch in Saugerties stayed apace with the new industrial-based wealth simply because the value of their land increased with the demand of its output. The farms of Saugerties fed the exponential increase of its non-farm population growth. In the post–Civil War census, Saugerties farms, still owned at the time by the original Dutch families, were valued far higher and had higher output than any other farms in Ulster County, and Saugerties had the highest population to feed of all Ulster County towns.

An enclave of "Yankee" culture had established itself in Malden by 1812 and was gaining wealth and influence from the tanning trade by the 1820s. Asa Bigelow from Connecticut had formed a merchant business and incorporated the village of Bristol there. Soon his wife's family, the Ishams, followed. After that, families their children had married into moved in, and by the 1830s, their combined numbers rivaled that of the earlier Dutch who surrounded them. Connections with the Yankee families who owned the large tanneries to the west through their Bristol Turnpike expanded their influence further into these mountain communities.

Asa Bigelow purchased the DeWolffen patent and the adjacent VanSteenberg farm, a combined five hundred acres of riverfront land hugging the deep channel of the Hudson, and made his improvements at Malden the most accessible for shipping in the area. His stores and those of the Ishams held a dominant position over all the trade of Saugerties from this river access. The first bluestone quarried by fellow Yankee Silas Brainard was shipped from these wharves. A multitude of new land routes destined for Malden spread like a web into the countryside.

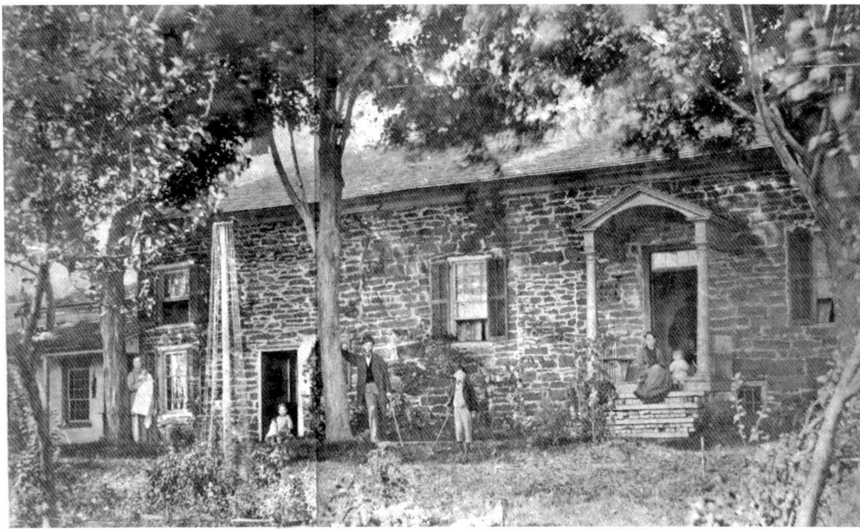

The 1712 riverfront Mynderse farmhouse was occupied in the 1880s by merchant Frederick Russell, whose wife was a Mynderse descendant. *Courtesy Fran Numrich.*

The bluestone industry had a relatively rapid start thanks to some highly proactive measures taken in Saugerties. The earliest bluestone sales were direct to dealers that had stone yards upriver at Coxsackie. At that same time, the early village records of Ulster (Saugerties) show an increase in its awareness of the infant bluestone trade and a desire to encourage it. It was closer to the quarries and was beginning to show this off with a legislated sidewalk and curb stone use. The first location for these pedestrian improvements was at Jeremiah Russell's store, before 1831, and had spread from there up Market Street, down Main Street and along Partition Street by 1833. The large population of the village of Ulster, its growing commercial presence and its frequent visitors attracted by the manufacturers allowed it a strong association with bluestone through this display. By 1837, William F. Russell had focused his father's business toward the direct purchase, sale and transport of bluestone, and in 1846, Jeremiah Russell purchased the Silas Brainard quarries and other lands north and south of this original site.

Bluestone Quarrying

Symbolically, in both a geological and economic sense, bluestone would become the foundation of Saugerties. Bluestone is the bedrock of the western two-thirds of Saugerties. The locations of the quarries in Saugerties made it economical to transport to market. Bluestone was a high-profit product because of the ease of quarrying it by hand. Its naturally occurring even seams of five- to seven-foot widths permitted the stone to be split into nearly square, smooth-surfaced, inch-and-a-half- to two-inch-thick slabs. Slabs of this thickness and dimension were highly marketable for sidewalks. Bluestone quarrying brought a new value to the land and a new source of income to the community.

Bluestone was not just quarried as flagstone for sidewalks but also as edge stone to be used for curbstones or window sills and headers. And it was quarried as rock—removed in massive four-inch to four-foot thicknesses to be later cut to order as building stone, doorsteps and porch platforms.

Bluestone is a unique material. The quality of its composition is what made it highly valuable. Its compactness and the fineness of its surface make it resistant to water and wear. These qualities were in great demand for sidewalks in all the growing cities of the Americas throughout the nineteenth century.

In the Saugerties area, the bluestone divides naturally into seams, or rifts, that follow a nearly true north–south direction. They occur between five and seven feet apart. A quarry often was started a dozen or more rifts from the exposed surface of the stone at the edge of a ledge to avoid the naturally formed headers.

The area to be quarried was cleared of its cover by blasting it away in the winter when its frozen overburden could be easily scraped from the smooth, flat bed of bluestone below.

The quarrying of bluestone follows a process distinct to its unique form and structure. Glaciation left the exposed ledges of bluestone lying like fanned cards where the spaces between the edges filled with soil and captured water. Bluestone quarries were first developed where bedrock was uncovered in this land between the ledges. The surface of the bluestone there had been kept wet by the water under the cover of soil, and this dampness prevented the natural cross seams, or headers, that formed where the bedrock was exposed. These quarries allowed larger, more valuable lifts to be productively taken because the size of the lift could be governed by drilling holes where a break was desired instead of being limited by naturally formed divisions.

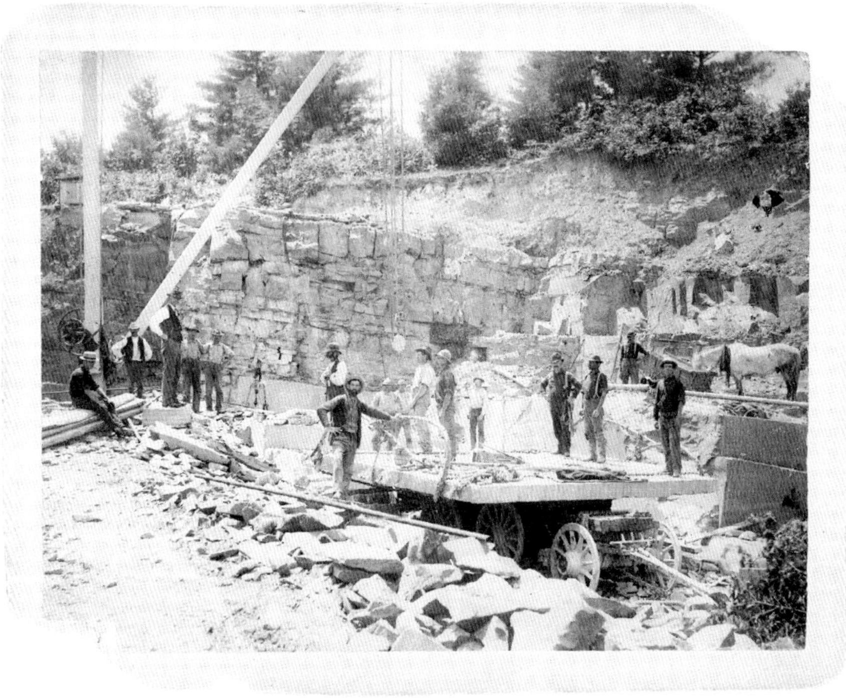

In the 1880s, the largest platform slabs went to New York City mansions on Fifth Avenue and were featured in news stories. *Author's collection.*

Quarries generated immense amounts of scrap stone called rubble. The chipped stone removed from the leading edge of a ledge to reach a speculative seam was dumped into large stacks a distance from the developing quarry over an unproductive part of the site. Waste was also accumulated in stacks as seams were exposed by blasting the frozen overburden. The material from the first broken cuts made to form the header for starting the quarry was also gathered into stacks. The larger quarries created entire shifts in the landscape as the rubble became hills or filled valleys.

Generally, quarrymen were not hired to work these sites. The land was leased to them, and they operated the quarries as partnerships or families in temporary communities that went from quarry to quarry. It was the Irish hard rock workers from the canals—who were experienced in cutting and finishing the stone of the dikes, dams and locks—who came to the quarries at first. In the earliest quarries, they not only extracted the stone but also finished it to marketable shapes and transported it to the dealer ready to be laid down as sidewalks. They were each their own craftsman and entrepreneur. Later, though, quarrymen transported their bluestone to the docks for finishing. This was because of a combination of factors. The first was that they were being paid by weight. But it is likely that many of the earlier skills had been lost after every farm and homestead began to mine their acreage for bluestone. This latter development led to the vast number of rubble mounds and prospecting pits found in the area of higher elevations. Most were unsuitable sites producing nothing but unmarketable stone fragments, but the number of quarrymen who were working these many sites made such a competition for a sale at the dock that the rush to the dock simply did not allow time for finishing the stone.

The quarrymen generally leased a site for 5 percent of the value of the bluestone they quarried. However, some dealers, such as John Maxwell, ran payrolls in the 1870s of up to $3,000 weekly, employing as many as eight hundred workers between the quarries and the finishing mills. At his peak, John Maxwell had a large fleet of sloops, schooners and steamers feeding his company wholesale yards in Rochester, Newark and Philadelphia.

Toward the end of the quarrying era, a quarryman working nine months a year was making around $300.00 annually delivering curbstone and slabs to the docks at about $2.00 per ton. When a skilled carpenter was making $2.50 a day, the average of three deliveries a week with an eight-ton wagon by comparison made quarrying a well-paying occupation for the time.

The Irish were more attracted by the availability of land they could purchase than the prospects of a lease. A vast amount of land had become available after the 1846 death of Robert L. Livingston. His two sons and heirs, Eugene and Montgomery Livingston, sold all the leased farmsteads they owned to their tenants. This represented all of the lands of the Woodstock Valley between Saugerties and Shandaken and the mountainsides that lined it. Irish quarrymen flocked to these mountainsides, where they could purchase speculative quarry sites from the former Livingston tenants in their uncultivated upland acres. Jeremiah Russell carried hundreds of loans as mortgage on these sites, and they paid off manyfold as the bluestone of Woodstock made the long trip over his Saugerties and Woodstock Turnpike to his docks on the Hudson.

Just as Jeremiah Russell developed quarry sites along his turnpike, the Bigelows similarly were supportive of quarrying along their Malden Turnpike at what would become Quarryville. Their turnpike soon spread the speculation to sites up into the road's mountain route in the Kaaterskill Clove. By mid-century, the three turnpikes of Saugerties—Glasco,

Saugerties and Woodstock and Malden—had become among the most active thoroughfares in the state, carrying an unending flow of bluestone from the quarries to tidewater. One eight-ton wagon at a time multiplied by hundreds, day after day, moved the hillsides of Saugerties to far-off cities as hundreds of thousands of flat, two-inch-thick slabs to pave their miles and miles of sidewalks.

Most of the landscape that would have been familiar to its inhabitants when Saugerties was born in 1811 was completely changed by the time Jeremiah Russell died in 1867. Hills were removed, ledges were flattened to become pasture and passages were opened between valleys. This, as it would turn out, would be only the beginning. Another half century of quarrying was yet to come, punctuated by ever-increasing output with the introduction of machines. By the early twentieth century, hardly a spot between upland Saugerties and the lower fringes of the Catskill Escarpment would be unscarred by an open quarry.

Bluestone brought continuous economic benefits to Saugerties over the first century of its life. This added a stable population base to its countryside, hamlets and village and, indirectly, also to its national exposure as both Jeremiah Russell and his son, William, were elected to Congress and the son of Asa Bigelow, John, became ambassador to France under President Lincoln.

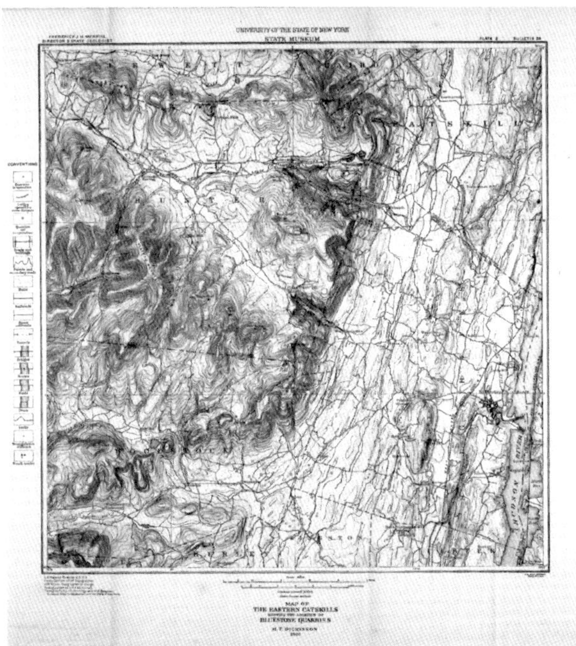

Bluestone quarrying was a major New York State industry with surveys that centered on the production in Saugerties. *From Bul. 59, NYS Museum, 1901.*

The natural potential of the resources of the countryside was first surveyed in 1609 with the journals of discovery of the voyages of Henry Hudson. They were again scientifically described in detail in an 1835 article for a publication called the *Zodiac*. This was done as a transit run from the base of the Catskill escarpment in a line to the Hudson River going straight through the breaks, or the falls, of the Esopus at Glenerie. Its analysis of the stresses on the rock that forms the cataract steps and the walls that form the break and gorge are the first speculation on record of the extinct glacial lake it calls Lake Albany.

There had been an early sawmill near the top of the breaks, but the cascades farther in and steep walls made the falls farther down nearly inaccessible. Colonel Edward Clark managed to overcome the challenge and set up his lead mill inside the gorge in 1831. James Eights, MD, the person doing the scientific study, writes in his article about Clark, his Great Falls Manufacturing Company and the atmosphere of a reclusive home he had created at what was called Glen Eirie, or eagles nest.

The Glenerie Lead Mill

Colonel Clark was a respected civil engineer with many inventions for such things as dry docks and canal locks. His early reputation began during the War of 1812, and his testimony is frequently found in the congressional record. He arrived in Saugerties in a wave of technically oriented people seeking the common ground Henry Barclay had cultivated here.

Edward Clark found Charles Ripley in Saugerties, and they decided to build a processing facility for making lead pigment and grinding it into oils in an oil refinery's empty mill building below Barclay's dam. John Eldridge, Robert L. Livingston's agent, had left this, the only one of the mills to be made of stone, sitting idle.

This was in the earliest of the shakedown period for applying the water to generating power to the iron and paper mills and the water was being rationed, so Clark decided he wanted to experiment with his own water works and began purchasing flood rights for a dam just where the Esopus comes out of the gorge into Barclay's Pond, at the second fall.

Meanwhile, Charles Ripley had attracted the interest of the Jewetts, established lead dealers in New York, for financing the enlargement of the old refinery, creating a rivalry between Ripley and Jewett's lead works and Clark's.

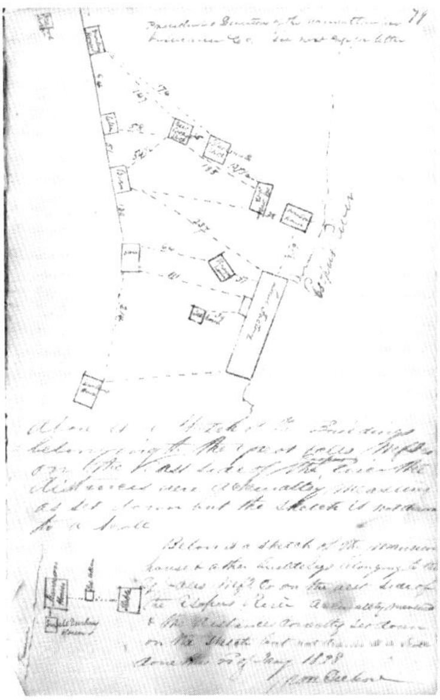

An 1830s layout of the lead mill at Glenerie sketched for an insurer on page 79 of Edward Clark's letter book. *Courtesy Christopher Evers.*

Clark had found that the natural dam at the lowest fall at the breaks had the drop and flow for the power he needed and could be made operational on the same schedule as his rival's expansion.

Recent information shows how quickly this took place. A surveyor's field book details a town road being laid out on both sides of the gorge between the Glasco Turnpike bridge and Clark's home and lead mill. This survey was done in April 1833, and Clark already had a house for himself built on the west side and the mill fully built on the east side of the Esopus Gorge.

James Eights, the naturalist who stayed with Edward Clark while writing the study published in 1835, marveled at the refinements Clark had made in his solitary Glenerie, including an iron-cable suspension bridge that spanned the entire gorge.

Clark and Henry Barclay were both in their early fifties at this time, and letter books that survive from both give insights into the pressures they both worked under—continually traveling for business to the city and dealing with transportation, material supply and post office difficulties. Both pressed through until nearly the same midcentury point when Edward Clark relinquished his business to Battelle and Renwick and moved to Brooklyn and Henry Barclay died. Both left the operations they started alive and well for the next several decades or more.

The legacy of Edward Clark's development of water power at the breaks is twofold. First, his manufacturing operations attracted transportation into this remote and solitary environment that eventually became the most direct route south to Kingston. Second, it brought interest in the location for its possibilities. In a development plan proposed in the 1890s, as water for the growing populations of cities created lucrative investment opportunities, the Ramapo Water Company surveyed for reestablishing a somewhat smaller Lake Albany by putting a dam in the breaks and plugging the Esopus back up again. That eventually was exactly what was done with the Esopus but to form the Ashokan reservoir several miles' distance upstream at West Shokan.

As for lead manufacturing at Saugerties, Charles Ripley unfortunately died within a few years of the beginning of this rivalry, but the patent claims continued to be argued between the Jewetts and Colonel Clark. Clark's methods remained productive for decades after the Jewetts' production in Saugerties ceased in the mid-1850s. A sizable community formed around the Glenerie lead mill that lasted until the last owner involved it in the Lead Trust in the 1890s and the works were consolidated into a larger location. In 1900, years before an arts colony was planned for Woodstock, a group of Boston investors sought to turn Glenerie into the Glen Eirie Workers, and this was promoted broadly in newspapers and in a custom booklet distributed in the United States and in England. That could have inspired Ralph Whitehead to come here, where he eventually created his Byrdcliffe colony at Woodstock to the west.

The term lead works is really a misnomer. Both inventors, Ripley and Clark, were concerned with making paint. It was not lead for pipes or for putty but oxidized to a powder suitable for marine and house paint. The principal reason for a chemical market in these early days was for the composition of paints, and Clark's product was as much an oil product as a lead product. Clark's main agent for sales was an old Nantucket whaling family who generations later would become Standard Oil. Battelle and Renwick's part in this stemmed from packaged paint, premixed in gallon barrels. They sold well in this business that had before sold pigment and mixing oils separately. When Colonel Clark had financial troubles, they took over the business immediately. The businesses they established from this product are still alive today. Paint in barrels was Clark's innovation. Years after he died, a patent for the re-sealable container exactly like that found today on the tar bucket lid was granted for his last application.

The estates of Barclay Heights, far above the deep gorge whose drop makes them heights, benefited from Clark and Ripley's relationship with the chemical industry. Edward Rising, who bought Clovelea right after W. R. Sheffield moved permanently to New York City, was in the industry, as were the Jewetts, who maintained a presence longer then their mill did. Cornelius Battelle had his residence looking over the pond and village. His daughter married Judge Vanderpoel, and they had their residence, Meadowside, overlooking the river. And of course, William Rhinelander Renwick and his main executive, John C. Steenken, added their family influence to the estate feel of Barclay Heights.

4

THE VILLAGE OF SAUGERTIES

Some of the most intriguing artifacts of the village of Saugerties' formative years are in a cabinet of Judge Charles Davis. In it are two maps of farms subdivided into lots: one called the Swart Farm and the other the Tjerck Schoonmaker farm. The Swart Farm is divided into streets and lots in this 1825 survey, and the Schoonmaker farm shows the same in 1828. Both are by the surveyor John Kiersted.

Both of these surveys are labeled with street names and are the first time these names are recorded in the village of Saugerties.

The Swart Farm had been purchased by Robert R. Livingston in 1803, and his brother, John, had constructed a store there as early as 1805. This is where Asa Bigelow set up his first business when he came from Connecticut, and left in 1810 to build the trade at Malden. It was the first place of business of Jeremiah Russell when he moved out of West Camp in 1814. When this subdivision map was created, the lot with that store was marked as George Gay's. That store was featured on period postcards as a drugstore and was still there forming the corner of Market and Main Streets in aerial photographs from 1955.

This survey borders on Main and Market Streets with Livingston Street through its center in the direction of a continuing Main Street to its left and the ancient road that would become the Saugerties and Woodstock Turnpike and today's Ulster Avenue to the right. Outside of the division lots, opposite them on the Main Street side, is a building sketch marking the Mynderse tavern with the name of its current occupant, James Woodruff. The symbol of a much more defined two-story house labeled J. Russel is on the opposite side of the subdivision. Far down at the end of Livingston Street is another symbol of a smaller house that is labeled T. Myer.

There are several iterations of this 1825 Livingston subdivision up to 1833. They add a school farther down on Main Street and the Brick Church when the congregation moved from Kaatsbaan into the growing village.

The Schoonmaker division is keyed to the Mynderse tavern, too, but by 1828, James Street ran along its side and was placed at this corner with Main. This map also names Jane Street, running parallel to Main Street. Partition Street is also drawn in and named, but the lots that are laid out face Main and Jane. Partition is not a commercial street at this time, and only large farm lots are shown fronting on it.

A cloth map by John Kiersted of 1825 has a larger area of divisions showing all the farms. In six years, this entire area would encompass the incorporated village of Ulster. The farms are marked with their owners' names. Among the sketched-in symbols for houses on each of these large parcels, the tight subdivision survey of the Swart farm stands out as the center of a future village.

Jeremiah Russell's brick store is located on this larger 1825 map as well as the landings for his sloops at the bottoms of Dock Street and Mynderse Street. His successful business was likely what put Livingston's village center where it was. Latching on to Henry Barclay's plans by selling most of the other land holdings to him made Livingston's earliest subdivision investment a prime mover in the idea of a village center.

By 1833, Jeremiah had already transferred the mercantile business to his son and son-in-law. By that time, business was closer to the mills, where the population growth was centered. That potential wasn't even imagined on Kiersted's map of 1825.

But by the end of the 1830s, the center of business shifted decisively back to Market Street as commercial bluestone quarrying developed along the turnpike that terminated there. Jeremiah Russell had become the financier of this new industry, and the company Russell & McCarthy; his son, William; and son-in-law, E.J. McCarthy, had shifted their operations toward marketing bluestone. In just a few years, the industrial traffic from the countryside along the turnpike so filled the widths of Market and Main Streets with commercial opportunities that these streets had become the commercial center of the entire town.

The residents of this area around Market Street controlled all the commerce in Saugerties and for a time held positions of power for the

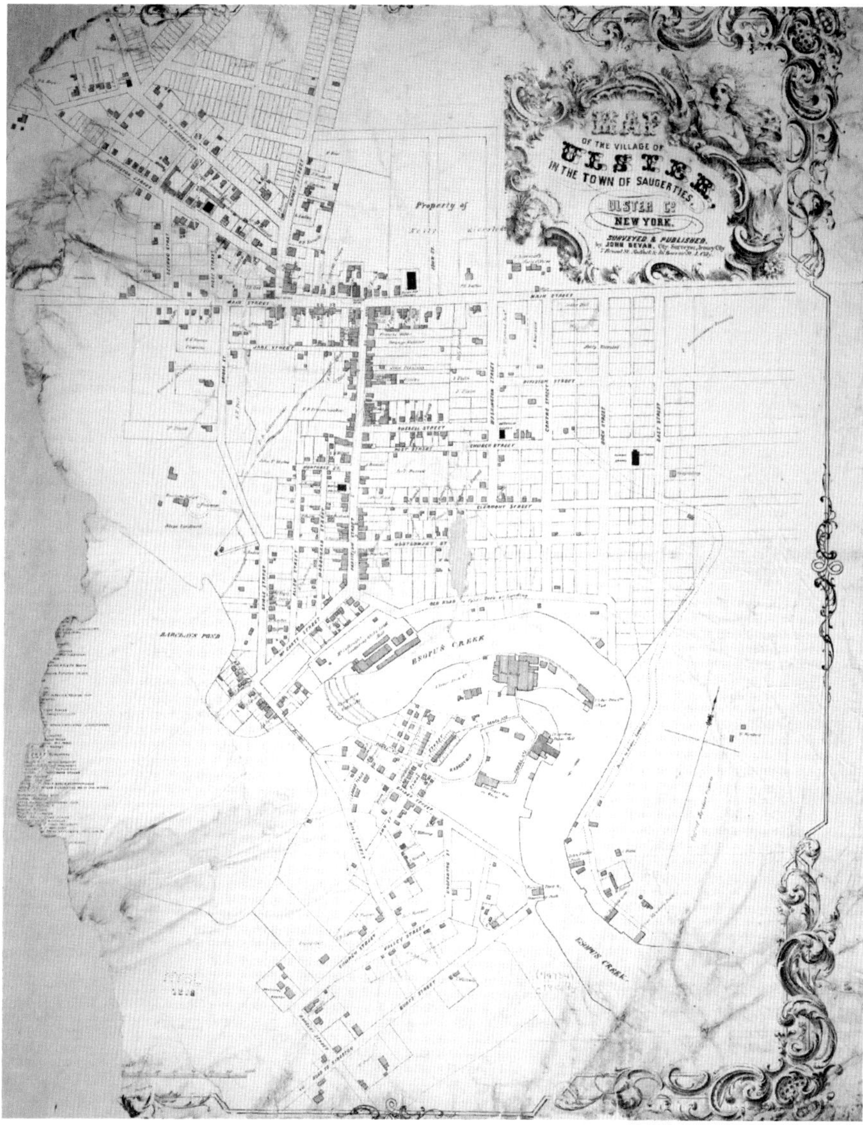

The twenty-year-old village of Ulster in an 1851 map before being renamed the village of Saugerties. *NYS Library special collections.*

broader region. Around their houses and merchant centers grew the early banking, social and political interactions of a village establishment.

What had been called Turnpike Street for most of this early growth of Saugerties village ended at Market Street, where William F. Russell's stately house still stands looking down the turnpike's center. On the right of this

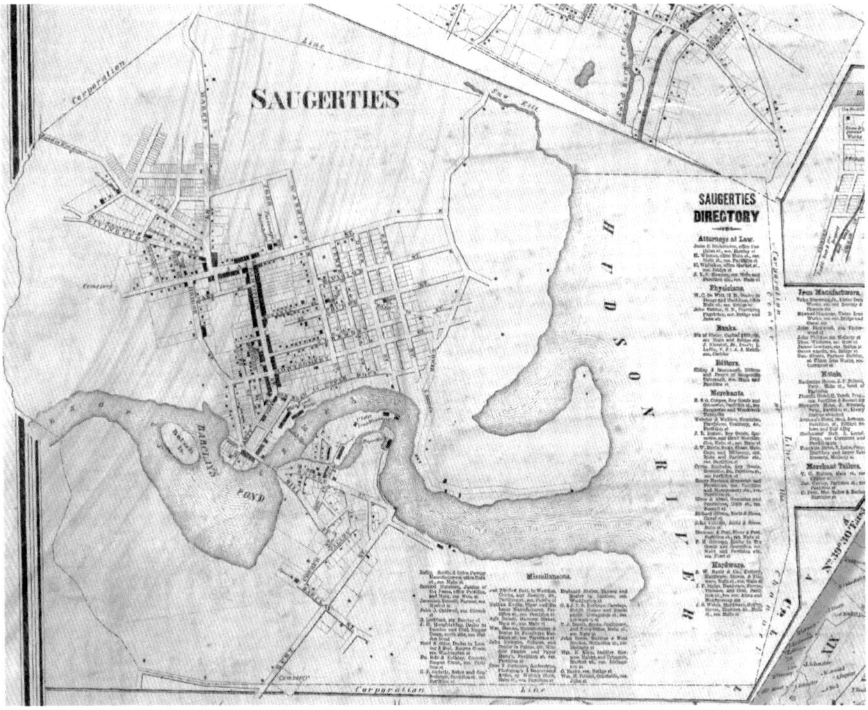

The 1858 French's wall map of Ulster County featured Saugerties in a dominant position and included with it its own business directory. *R&L Archive collection.*

view is the large 1814 frame house of Jeremiah Russell with its two-tiered, columned porch facing his son's house across what was once a village green. Across the turnpike is the Dutch gabled house of Jeremiah's other son David, captain of the sloop *Livingston* and a major bluestone dealer in the earliest days of its sales in 1836. All three of these houses sat on grounds that provide open views of the village on one side and extensive farms with the Catskill Mountains in the distance on the other.

Just down Market Street from William F. Russell's house was Luther Laflin's comfortable estate house. This stood until the 1960s, when it was replaced by a bank. It was within the space that associated it with the Russells, in a row of half a dozen estate houses that extended down Market Street. As time went on, Luther's son, Fordyce, built his estate house to occupy a whole block on Main Street between John and Washington. Colonel H. Dwight Laflin, Luther's other son, would have his estate house at the head of West Bridge Street. The large estate houses of Laflin sons-in-law and other relations basically established the village side streets, as this family-run business grew ever more successful, rivaling DuPont before the Civil War.

The Russell houses were modest compared to the Laflins', who would set the tone for the style of the village. When Saugerties reached its centennial in 1911, H.D., at eighty-three, led the parade. From what's to be found in the *Old Home Week* program, one doesn't imagine there is anything that was *home* outside of the townhouses that lined the streets that branched off Main and Partition Streets, the then nucleus of the village of Saugerties. Most of the rest of the town in its own celebration was decidedly unrecognized.

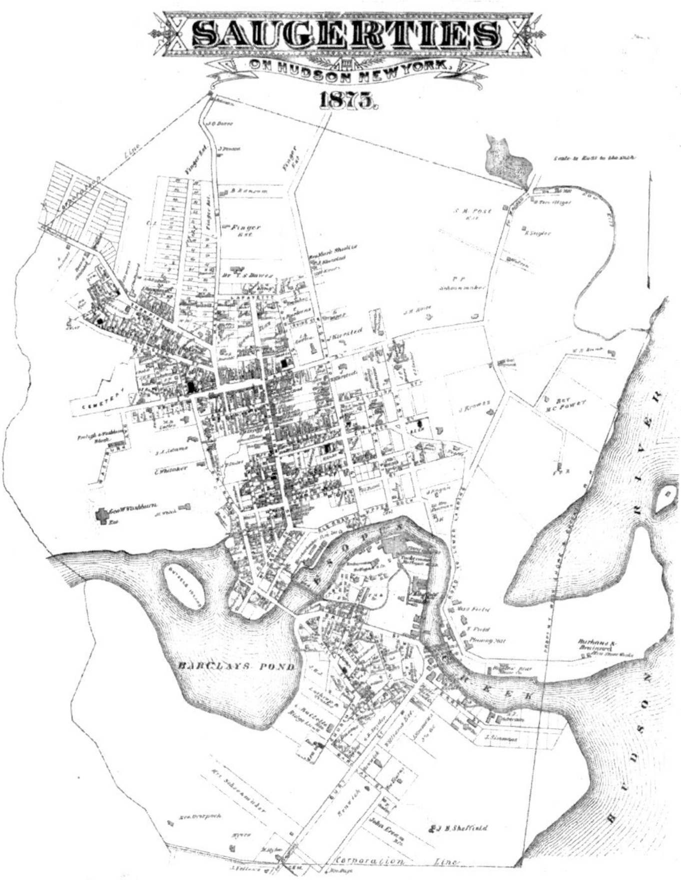

The 1875 *Beers Atlas of Ulster County* devoted double-page spreads to both the north and south village, which are combined together here. *Author's collection.*

The Laflins arrived with the first wave of manufacturers and first lived far down 9W outside of the Barclay Heights neighborhood. Winthrop Laflin was involved in the largest paper manufacturing firm in Massachusetts in 1829 when his brother, Matthew, came to Saugerties to purchase from Henry Barclay a mill site for manufacturing axes. That site was directly beside the new machines of Barclay's paper mill, and everyone knew axes weren't the primary business of a Laflin.

By 1831, Matthew had accomplished what he came for, but he had gotten used to the place and his attention was drawn to an opportunity that he felt worth speculating in. About the same time Edward Clark was setting up his lead manufacturing at Glenerie, Matthew Laflin also moved into the remote reaches of the countryside to set up mills to manufacture gunpowder on the Plattekill and Cauterskill Creeks.

Both Clark and Laflin recognized productive uses for native materials abundant in the countryside. Clark used vinegar for corroding lead into powder. Laflin used manure and urine to make phosphorus to mix with the native charcoal, also long produced by the settlers of the town. Their processes gave both Clark and the Laflins more of an opportunity to be personally involved with the country population than any of the other recent arrivals of the village. The Laflins were most popular because they employed so many in the mills and so many more making barrels, teaming the product to the magazines built near the river and supporting the quarrying of bluestone with the powder used to remove top burden from the bedrock. Of all the manufacturers, they were most recognized as supplying the greatest benefit to the community.

Matthew's brothers Winthrop and Luther and Luther's brother-in-law, Solomon Smith, had come from Massachusetts over the course of the 1830s as the Laflin business increased. By the time the Laflins began to show the extent of their wealth by building their village residences, the generation of Fordyce L. and H. Dwight Laflin was being groomed to run a business that was fast adding manufacturing plants across the United States and into Canada. Their choice to keep their home base not just in Saugerties but in the area of the village around Main Street gave them the goodwill of the business sector there for the next half century and more.

The Laflins supplied the example needed for merchants to build new residences as well as new commercial buildings that spread over the village, where farmsteads and scattered roadside stores and taverns had been the norm. This was not done alone. Successful farmers and quarry operators from the countryside found this was the way to show they were also

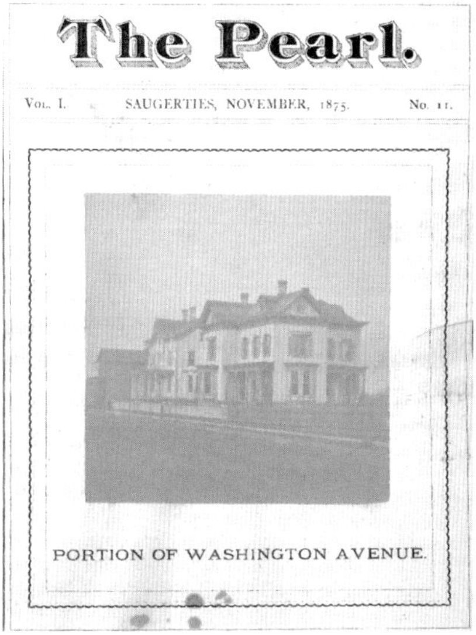

Houses first began appearing outside the village center after the Civil War and were the homes of merchants like Egbert Cooper. *Courtesy Audrey Klinkenberg.*

established. In the decade following the Civil War, a pace of building was set that expanded the street system in a growth pattern that would go on for the next eighty years. The grand houses of the Van Etten, Seamon, Maxwell, Blackwell, Cantine, Cooper and Davis families all were initially influenced by the Laflins.

These residences were not periodically occupied as townhouses. The Laflins had set the example by living in their homes off of their wealth, being attentive to their businesses while also being patrons of the local saloons and dress shops and tobacconists in a village that was a public extension of their personal living space.

The population that emulated this Laflin lifestyle created a completely new level of clientele for the stores of Main and Partition Streets in the years before the turn of the century. Shop owners began to demand styles in the architecture of their buildings and seek out decor and merchandise for their businesses that was attractive to this more refined taste. This spread along Main and Partition Streets and soon developed into an entire village where the local origin of wealth was displayed in the patronage of businesses.

The Victorian era was in full bloom, and welcoming porches and door yards allowed the residents of the village's houses to extend their greetings to the strollers on the promenade-width sidewalks that had become the main feature of every civilized urban scene by that time. As a sign of this gentrification, ordinances that required wide tire widths on the massive bluestone wagons allowed the tram stone reminders of rural roads to be removed from the village's main streets. With the arrival of the railroad station, this part of the town was annexed to the village, and the expense of improving the ancient terminus of the turnpike brought its length into full compliance with the paving standards of the rest of the village. The turnpike was transformed into Ulster Avenue.

On Main Street, first the Davis store was laid out as a sidewalk-exposure environment, showing its interior shopping experience through large panes of glass. Then the Whitaker Block went up with its stylish cornice four tall stories above the street. It was followed by the Russell Block with even more glass area, height and expanse along both Market and Main Streets. As the remaining space for storefronts became less available, the stylish iron fronts were employed to renew older buildings to attract the gentry.

All of these changes can be observed as they happened starting with Jernegan's photos of 1875 for *The Pearl* and, later, by De Lisser for his *Picturesque Ulster of 1905*. A multitude of postcards from the height of their popularity, between 1890 and the late 1910s, fills the image gap and extends the height of the village center to its climax in the era of the Kodak. Large gable-front frame stores were replaced by the multistoried brick structures that dwarfed them, and then the remaining antiquated stores' spaces were replaced with designs to carry a cadence of windows and doors and walls that climbed to fill a unified skyline. This effect was still intact when aerial photos captured all angles of the business district in 1955.

A full-page article in the *New York World* in 1889—illustrated with a sampling of the great houses, including H. D. Laflin's and William Sheffield's, and a tour-style map—sang the praises of this "city"—not that it meant to imply it was a city but that it had the sophisticated air of a city. That impression remains where these commercial buildings and side-street residences survive today as they battle a present reality that is unguided by such polished expectations.

This business district part of the village of Saugerties was accepted as a landmark in the National Register of Historic Places in 1982. By that time, it had been taken for granted for so long that it, and the entire village, was beginning to be treated as ordinary. The pace of the twentieth century set by the windshield view from an automobile left an attitude that this village was no different from thousands of downtowns in the experience of the vast traveling public.

Saugerties suffered from this image doubly. Its business district is a merging place for one federal and two major state highways. Added to that is the singularly unique position of having the Esopus Creek gorge's terrain and only one bridge crossing it to carry two of these roads.

By midcentury, highway traffic had become the focus of business interests. Service stations and parking lots began then to fill the open spaces and replace the few residences left along the commercial blocks. Once the Thruway opened, two of the venerable Laflin estates made way for a supermarket

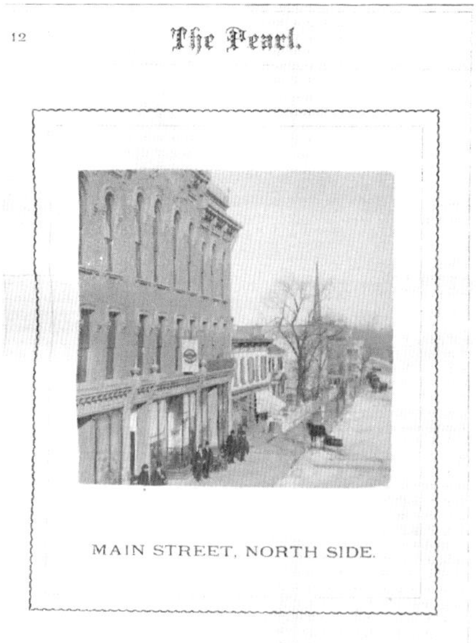

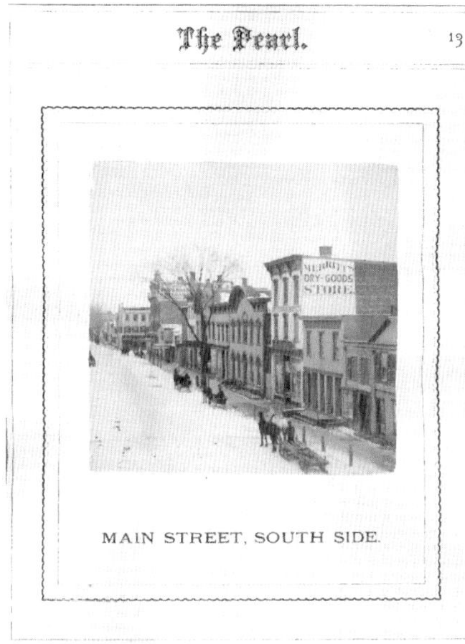

Left: The north side of Main Street in 1875 with the new Russell Block building at the corner of Market Street. *Courtesy Audrey Klinkenberg. Right*: The south side of Main Street in 1875 with the new Whitaker Block in the distance toward the corner of Partition Street. *Courtesy Audrey Klinkenberg.*

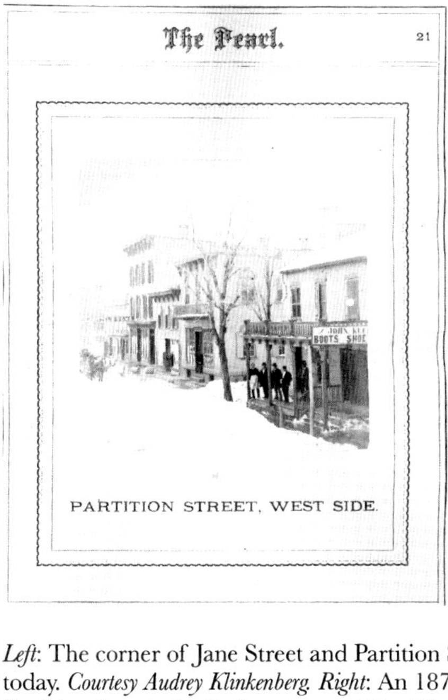

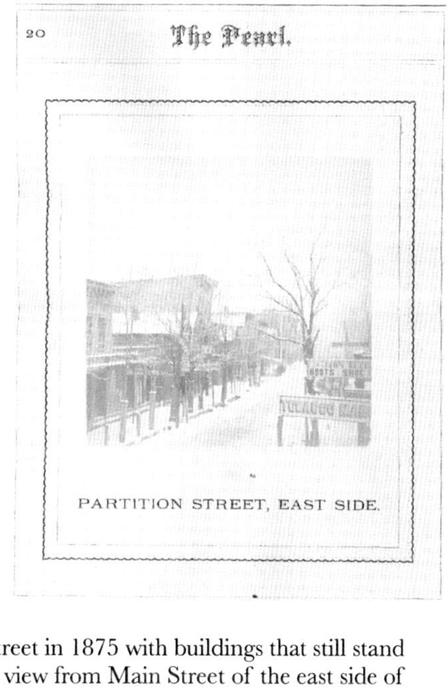

Left: The corner of Jane Street and Partition Street in 1875 with buildings that still stand today. *Courtesy Audrey Klinkenberg. Right*: An 1875 view from Main Street of the east side of Partition Street with its farm-lane width still as narrow today. *Courtesy Audrey Klinkenberg.*

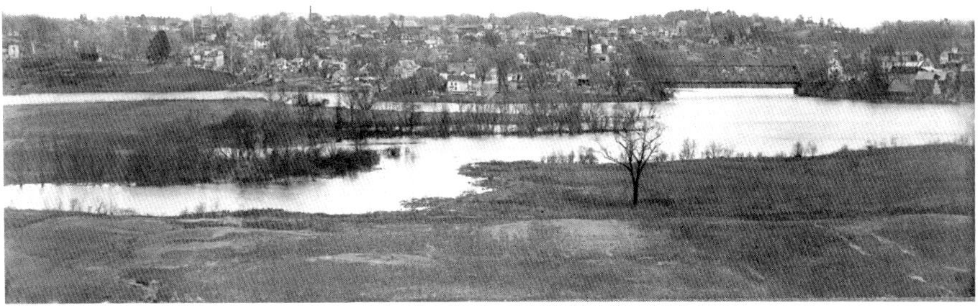

An early 1900s panorama of the village's south slope in the area of Henry Barclay's original 1827 "model village" plan. *From Jeanne Goldberg.*

and a gas station. Into the 1960s, a score of iconic commercial structures were demolished so parking lots could keep the downtown competitive with the new shopping centers.

Excluding the grids of residential districts that filled every large farm within walking distance of the village during this period, the basic street map of the village center has changed little in two hundred years. The village was featured as an enlarged detail on the wall-size county maps of 1853 and 1858 and rates two double-page spreads in the 1875 *Beers Atlas of Ulster County*. The importance of roads converging on a geographic feature and the services clustered there for the convenience of travelers had always explained the prominence of the village of Saugerties. It is where roads met steamboats and trains and the bridge that is there to connect it all.

Catskill up the river and Rondout to the south were similar transportation hubs for the same reason, but only Saugerties had the King's Highway so near to the river and, later, to the railroad. So when the Thruway took the course of the King's Highway and subdivisions grew across the village's bridge, the demands placed on all of Saugerties' important heritage assets were extreme.

None of the basic geographic factors that caused the village center to grow where it did are different from the days when it was known as Saugerties-on-Hudson. It is still a transportation hub with residential neighborhoods surrounding a downtown for the purpose of supporting whatever this hub motif may draw. But the factors that attract what it draws have changed significantly.

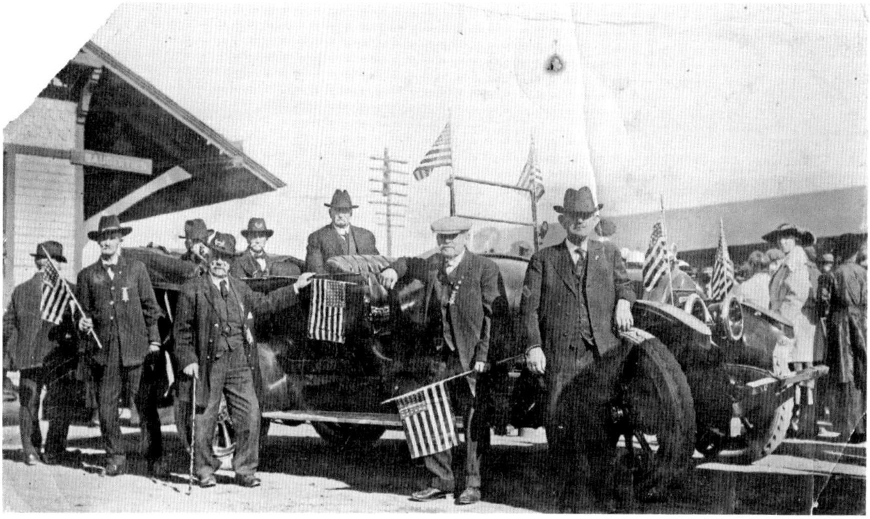

After the railroad arrived, dignitaries were greeted at the train station and sidewalks were created along Ulster Avenue leading to it. *Courtesy Melanie Gardner.*

Of all that represents the ghostly image of Saugerties' past in ancient postcards and published photographs from the past century and a half, only the landmark structures of the historic business district remain as a public display to continue a heritage. This is the pride of Saugerties and its identity. The steamboats are gone. The railroad doesn't stop here. The mills have gone. The estates, to the extent that they are identifiable with the patriarchs of the community, have gone.

There is an estranged relationship with history that is most pronounced in a resistance to accept responsibility for this identity with the past. There is a nearly universally recognized historic business district in Saugerties, one of the first in the state. A timidity that has been bred in three generations of avoidance that bows to the interests of a few undeveloped, unprepared and opportunistic occupants of historic structures is all that can now threaten the true character of the village of Saugerties.

5

A COMMUNITY LOST TO HISTORY

It is said that Henry Barclay named his house Ury after the ancestral home of his family in Scotland. But the 1834 record of informal villages in New York lists Ury as a separate place from the formal village of Ulster, now the village of Saugerties. There were marriage, death and society announcements in New York City papers from the 1830s with their location as Ury. Ury was a whole community's location, not a single address, and took up the entire part of Barclay Heights that falls within the bounds of the village today. It was like Gramercy Park to Manhattan or Brooklyn Heights to Brooklyn.

On an 1825 survey map, what would be Ury was just a winding road and four houses with barns. The earliest public statement of Henry Barclay's intent, in February 1826, gave the advantages of a high state of cultivation of the land when describing the site of his Woodstock and Saugerties General Manufacturing and Mining Co. Given the open-field agricultural practices of the time, most of the water rights he purchased were on large areas of farmland. There would have been expansive views for, in the Dutch vernacular, a *streak*—as far as the eye could see. Imagine looking down 9W today from the turn at the Knights of Columbus Hall. That long, level view would have been 360 degrees around. That was the great open space that Ury had in the second quarter of the nineteenth century.

In the first few years, the mills were the priority. The old Dutch farmhouses were all that was needed or used in what would be Ury. According to the 1918 reminiscence of a longtime resident, Henry Barclay lived in an old

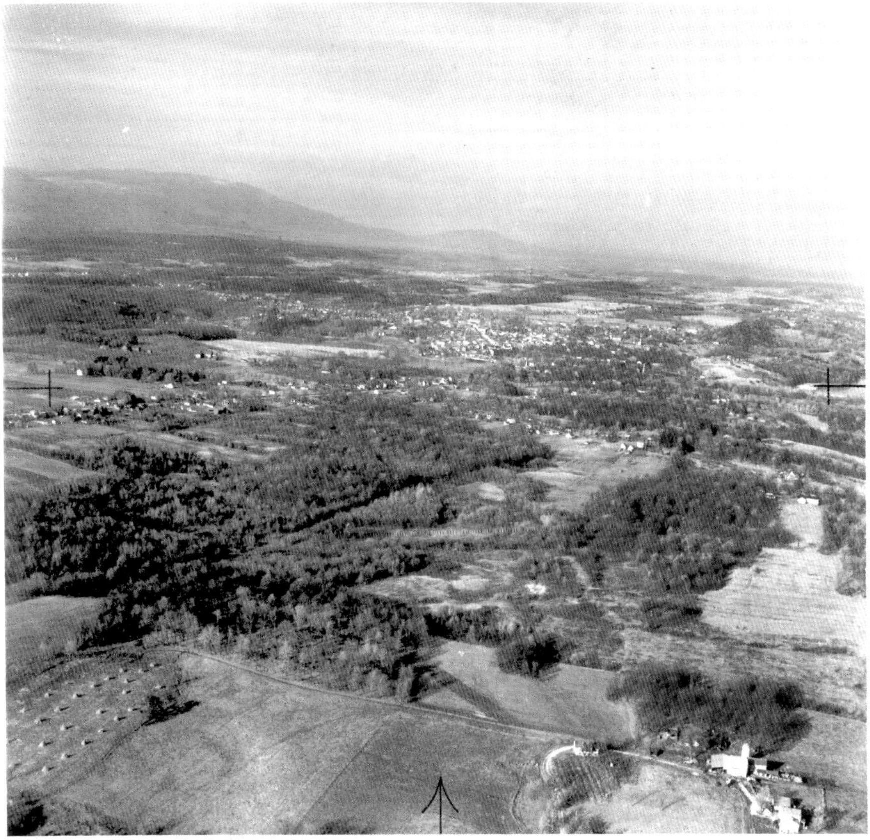

By 1955, the open fields between Barclay Heights and Glasco were experiencing their first overgrowth since the earliest colonial farms. *R&L Archive collection.*

farmhouse at the end of Barclay Street, and Moses Yale Beach lived in the old farmhouse at the end of Beach Street. The Mansion House (now the Knights of Columbus Hall) was the first new structure. It was built as a boardinghouse to accommodate those visiting, becoming involved in or purchasing in the area and for those setting up the technology in the mills. There were over forty rooms constantly buzzing with the technically skilled, enthusiastic and curious.

By the mid-1830s, the front line of Ury, occupying the ridge overlooking the Esopus Harbor, was filled with the evenly spaced new homes of Barclay and Kearney, the Mansion House, the Trinity Church and the home of Theodore Barrell. More than the mills themselves, these five large structures, along the edge of their high perch, alerted travelers on the Hudson to

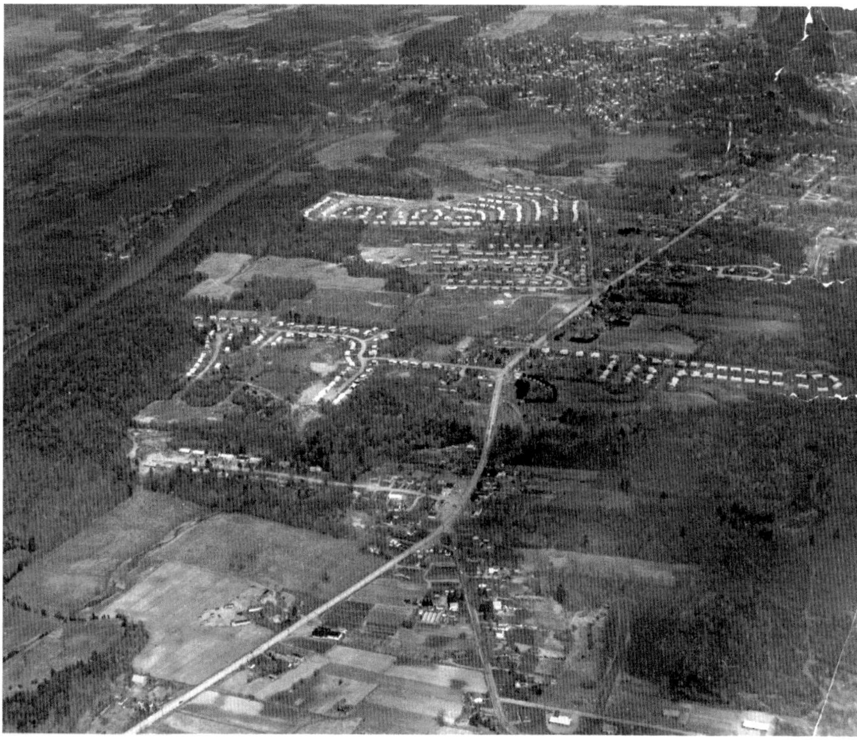

By 1965, the dairy farms between Barclay Heights and Glasco that still had open fields had been covered with housing developments. *R&L Archive collection.*

investment that was being made in Saugerties. Their position reflected the vision of those doing this investment. The bright white of their painted walls sent the message that there was clarity of thought, unity and success here. (And of course, that we also made white paint here.)

Ury was Saugerties's cultural center. It looked across at the village of Ulster and out on the waters and the distant mountains. It oversaw the iron, paper and other industries built below. It was a special reserve for those who appreciated their achievements together. Ury was the destination for those curious about Saugerties. For three generations, if you thought creatively or drove innovation, Ury was the destination of your pilgrimage. The focus of industry may have been on the waters that visually surrounded this place, but thoughts naturally took in the long view over the horizons. The open fields and high prospect made Ury a place for seeing the present and contemplating the future.

Barclay Heights

Ury is the visible symbol of a social contract. There had been an agreement from the earliest planning of Ury. It may be codified in only one reference that is known and in a single deed restriction, but its presence is palpably clear. It only takes verbal form in the early 1870s, when the farms that had always kept the fields cultivated south of Trinity Cemetery were beginning to break up the large tracts that had not changed since the town of Saugerties was formed. It was then that the estates joined together and bought the area they called the meadow, the land between the cemetery and the land Henry Barclay's estate had sectioned off as lots but that William Rhinelander Renwick combined back together to keep the space open.

John Simmons had acquired all the land surrounding Trinity Church on its south for a similar purpose. The only *new* additions to Ury are Clovelea on lots 13 and 14 of the Barclay auction map that John Simmons sold to W.R. Sheffield in 1876, and the Gables that Anna and Francis Steenken built on lots 11 and 12 in 1913 that they bought from the Simmons family. For the Gables, the deed specified that the house be only one story in order not to block the view. The architect, Henry Corse, designed the house to be angled so that the added floor space of a sprawling one-story house did not form a wall to this sense of openness.

The Corse design for the Steenken house was the last great house to share the ridge surrounding the open commons of Ury. Meadowside; Brightbank; Clifton; Burtt House; Mansion House; the houses of Corse, Bigelow, Tuckerman, Mulligan, Beach, Battelle, Barrell and Young's Inglewood; the Trinity Church; and, finally, the Gables and Clovelea all looked out on each other's views across a common meadow. That feeling of civilized sharing was intact even as late as 1955, when the aerial photographs Morris Rosenblum took capture Ury nested on the edge of Barclay Heights.

The brick and granite Brightbank, built by Blase Lorrilard on the site of Henry Barclay's comparatively humble frame 1826 mansion house in 1855, was where the Sheffield family called home until its 1892 sale to Robert Main, an international dealer in brick. In the twentieth century, it was one of the houses of the Reverend Edwin Jan Van Etten of Boston, who was known for delivering the first religious programming on the first commercial radio station in 1921. He made the house into a sanatorium during World War II and sold it to Ruth Dale in 1943. In 1967, it was made into apartments.

This was happening with all of the great estates of Ury toward mid-century. When in 1949 Clovelea became the Stonewall Hotel and later

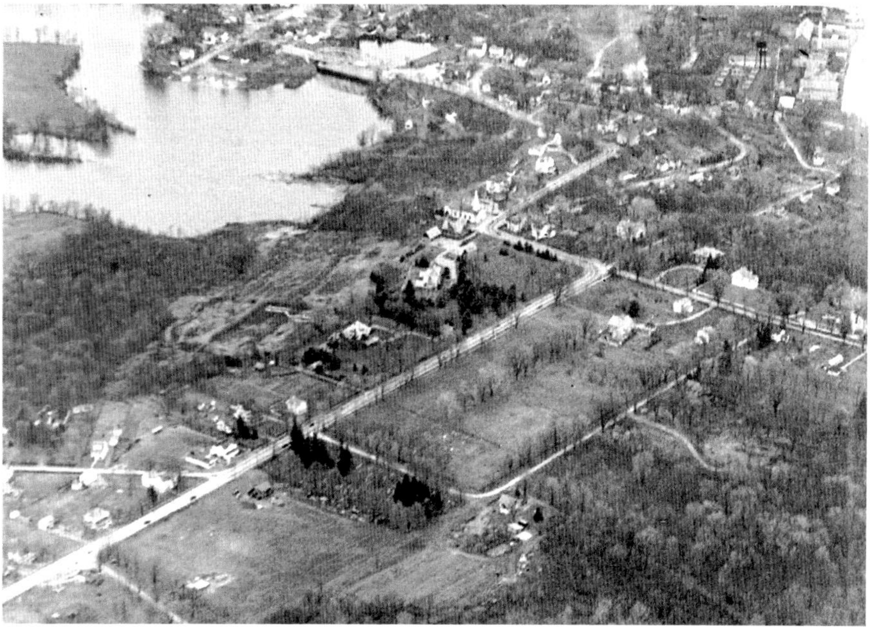

Common meadows in the middle of open-lawned estates on Barclay Heights were still maintained in the early 1950s. *R&L Archive collection.*

Antons and then the Dragon Inn, it had joined Brightbank, whose last owner felt its space was better suited during the war as a sanatorium. The fate of all the showcase homes of Ury followed the same trends that justified the displacement of a heritage identity that the urban renewal fever of the time, essentially no different than the communizing of culture in communist societies of the age, was encouraging in government programs.

Meadowside, the summer retreat of the Vanderpoels, who gave the Morris window to Trinity Church in 1873, was the land in Ury that initiated the subdivision trend that eventually crept over all of Barclay Heights. In 1953, it was divided into building lots.

Mansion House, sometimes called Hillcrest, is now occupied by the local Knights of Columbus. The last to use it as a residence was Evelyn Wachter, who was the last Simmons descendant to own it. It had been a boardinghouse, a school and a residence since it was built possibly as early as 1826.

Of the same vintage is Clifton, which, today, as a bed and breakfast, is called the Renwick Clifton house. It alone has bucked the trend for the earliest of these mansions in its restoration to close to original condition. It was originally built by John Watts Kearney, who arrived with Henry

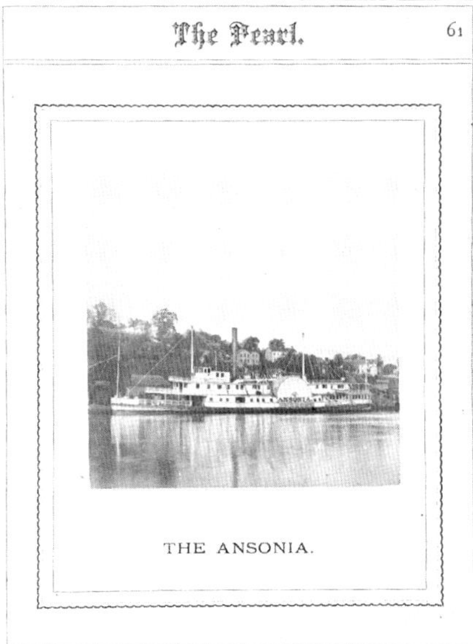

In the days of steamboat travel, the *Ansonia* was a short walk downhill and Barclay Heights a short ride from Manhattan. *Courtesy Audrey Klinkenberg.*

Barclay and made Ury the home where he raised his sixteen children. Kearney's connections were responsible for the long list of historical figures that spent time in Ury over those early decades. Kearney and Barclay were married to sisters. Since the Barclays had no children and the Kearneys had twelve and then John had four more after his first wife died, the neighboring households were always a busy place. Eliza Hammeken, John's second wife, occupied the house well into the 1890s, after which it was purchased by Edmund Hurry, the son-in-law of William R. Renwick. Hurrys occupied it for the next century.

The house that George Hammeken built was replaced by John T. Washburn in the style of the late 1910s, and only a fleeting glance at an old photo shows the house that was the one William Burtt while manager of the iron works and then William Rhinelander Renwick lived in while overseeing the lead mill in Glenerie and the *Ansonia* for his Saugerties Transportation Company. It is important to recognize that each of these homes was one of many that their owners occupied. Each kept a townhouse in Manhattan or Brooklyn and, in the case of Renwick, homes near the chemical refineries of the company in New Jersey.

Cornelius Battelle had the cottage on the inside corner where Church Street turns into Hill Street. He was William R. Renwick's partner. In 1846, Battelle married Catherine Barclay Kearney, one of John Watts Kearney's daughters, at Ury. When she died in childbirth, the child was raised by the Kearneys. This child later married Judge Vanderpoel and they built Meadowside. Battelle could be considered a prototype industry lobbyist and spent most of his time at his home in Washington, D.C. Though Saugerties relates Battelle and Renwick to mostly local concerns, divisions of their original chemical company were beginning after the Civil War to be what they remain today: national leaders in the fields of research and specialized transport.

In the early years before Barclay, the only house occupying this high point was the old Schoonmaker farmhouse. Beside this, Moses Yale Beach built a stylish brick house with a Greek-columned porch that overlooked the Esopus outlet and the river. Beach is one of three, with George Hammeken and John Kearney, credited with operating the first Fourdrinier machine for making paper in America. The Smithsonian documents this happening in Saugerties in 1827. By 1832, Beach was an early village trustee and had also founded the first fire department. By 1836, he had left Saugerties to take over the *New York Sun* newspaper from his brother-in-law, Benjamin Day. In 1848, he founded the Associated Press. His son, who spent his youth in Ury, ran the *Sun* after his father retired, founded *Scientific American* and engineered the first experimental subway, the pneumatic subway, in New York.

Moses Yale Beach came to Saugerties around 1828 in his late twenties to apply a pulp-making machine he'd invented by involving it with Barclay's machinery from England to help support the manufacture of the first machine-made paper in America. He'd run into financial trouble pioneering a steamboat route to supply rag for papermaking from the textile mills of New England and came to Saugerties for a second chance at making a business from his invention.

When Beach left Saugerties, he famously retained a connection between the mills and the *Sun* by using its offices as a discount center in New York City for redeeming Saugerties bank notes (shin plaster) during the Free Banking Era from 1837 to 1862. Curiously, most of the information on this activity and the early exploits of Moses Yale Beach comes from the incessant belittlements of his character published by his rival newspapermen James Gordon Bennett of the *Herald* and Horace Greeley of the *Tribune*, who painted Beach's life as an inventor and entrepreneur as failures in an effort to destroy his credibility with the working-class readership they all sought. Their strongest jabs were directed against the *Sun* as a redemption place for the shin plaster of Jeremiah and William F. Russell's banking interests in Saugerties.

It is interesting to note from these accounts that the discount on redemption of Saugerties shin plaster was one of the lowest of the period. This meant there was greater faith in the currency of the banks of this thriving industrial center than in centers of more populist forms of economic development such as mines and agriculture. It may be speculated that it was the consistent high exchange rate of Saugerties bucks before midcentury and the savvy of smart people like Moses Yale Beach that turned the tide toward industrialization for the rest of the country at the beginning of the next half of the nineteenth century.

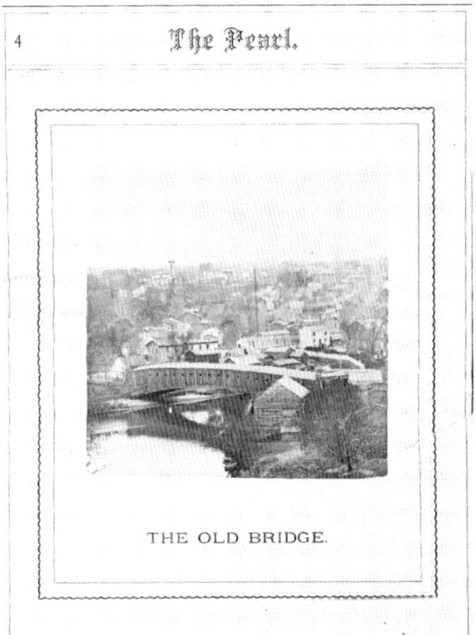
4 The Pearl.

THE OLD BRIDGE.

The Esopus at Saugerties was first bridged in 1831, but the 1840 covered bridge designed by Ralph Bigelow is its classic representation. *Courtesy Audrey Klinkenberg.*

Between Battelle's and Beach's homes were the matching houses of the iron works owners Tuckerman and Mulligan, and farther toward the Trinity Church was the house of William Young, the first manager of the iron works. In 1831, Young had built his house on the heights overlooking the pond to set himself above, so to speak, the manager's stately stone house with its columned portico built as the centerpiece of the mill-side community of stone row houses Henry Barclay had designed to emulate a model European village plan of the period. Burtt made the same decision in the 1840s, and Tuckerman and then Mulligan followed suit in the '50s and '60s. The desire to have the biblical house on the hill was a strong element in the identity of Ury. Mulligan, the last owner of the Ulster Iron Works, occupied Brightbank at the time he sold the iron works to William Sheffield.

The longest-living resident along this ridge in 1917 was Margaret Winslow in the house her grandfather Theodore Barrell built three years before Trinity Church was erected. He and his Italian son-in-law, Ferdinand Messa, along with James Morgan Ashley, used a booming Saugerties to test out retailing schemes. Barrell was settling into a retirement after a long career in trade in South America. He was an old friend and associate of Henry Barclay from Barclay's earlier career in the merchant assurance business.

Of the three townhouses fronting on Barclay Street, the oldest is Ralph Bigelow's. He designed and built the Trinity Church in 1831 and the Burr arch covered bridge in 1840, and this house is from that period. He came from Chatham, up the river, where they celebrate him for the design and building of the church there when he was a teenage prodigy. That community published an account of his career as one of the most prominent builders in New York City for his obituary at the turn of the century. The house he built in Ury is the middle one of the three townhouses that once lined this stretch of Barclay Street. The Simmons house that was on the corner of Valley Street was destroyed sometime in the 1970s. The house beside the Mansion House was part of this property when it was built by G.K. Snyder, the owner of the Saugerties and New York Steamboat Company.

The Steenkens lived in Ury in the house built by Henry Barclay in a Spanish style for Mrs. Lovina Deas in the 1830s. Deas was the heiress to a large plantation in Virginia and settled in Ury after divesting herself of its slave holdings. Her husband was a sea captain, and he was part of a long list of visitors, relatives and residents of Ury who were all acclaimed for their exploits in military actions and foreign relations before midcentury. The contacts between Ury and Texas, Mexico, California and the border states were especially strong. Stephen Kearney, John Watts Kearney's younger brother, was the first governor of California, and George Hammeken, John's father-in-law, built the earliest railroads in Mexico and Texas. Moses Yale Beach used these early Ury connections for his logistics when he established the Associated Press during the Mexican War.

John G. Steenken ran the Glenerie Lead Works for Renwick and Battelle and owned it when it was merged into the lead trust. When he died, his daughters built the house that is between Trinity Church and Clovelea, the Gables. It was designed by Henry Corse, whose family's house, the Ralph Bigelow house, overlooked the always-open meadow where the house was being planned. He traveled to England to study examples of the picturesque style practiced there to make the house blend into the landscape. In the 1920s, this estate became occupied by Charles F. C. Mehlig, an inventor of dental surgical devices.

The estates of Barclay Heights retained an exclusivity in their relationship to the village, while the history of the countryside had to wait before it could emulate this use of the land of Saugerties.

In the early days of bluestone quarrying, as the landscape of Saugerties inexorably shifted ton by ton down the river, the wetlands and meadows nested between rocky ridges, prized for cattle grazing, expanded. The rubble left from the quarrying was spread and covered, with the soil overburden always set aside for reclaiming the land. The land use for agriculture was the greatest concern in the decades before and after the Civil War, and quarried land was made whole again.

Today, a level field that does not support tall growth is a sign that an early quarry has been returned to useful grazing land; a high mound of loose stone fragments near the face of a ridge means restoring the land was no longer a concern. The mounds are all at quarries from the 1890s on to the

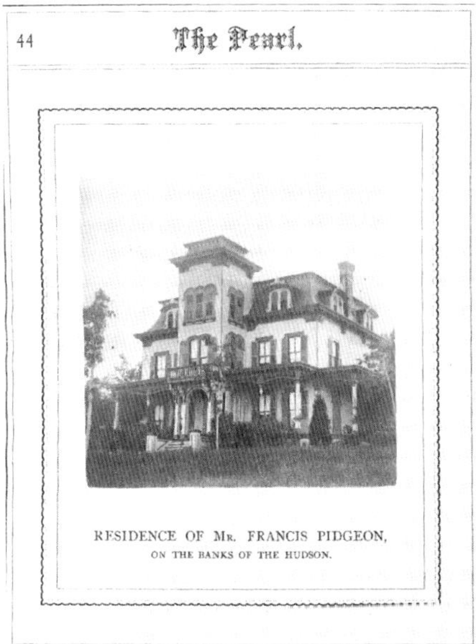

Estate houses lined the river and every other place possessing a view after the Civil War, and that continues to this day. *Courtesy Audrey Klinkenberg.*

decline of the market in the 1930s. They are a sign of quarrying's economic success as the bluestone product of the countryside so discouraged the traditional free grazing of cattle into the woodland meadows that this had ceased as a commonplace practice and there was no longer an economic reason to reclaim the land.

In the earliest days, the countryside still used every acre to feed the industrial village. But when money was to be made from the small plots where the quarryman's family lived, fed themselves and operated their own quarry, the use of the land turned into hundreds of residential plots. What land was once used for grazing was fenced, and herds declined. By 1900, the two-hundred-year-old tradition of husbandry had been lost.

Only gentleman farms could have bucolic fields with grazing herds. Brightbank was one under John Main's tenure and had enough families living there to make up the population of a countryside hamlet. Stroomzeit—under the residency of Frank Pidgeon, then John G. Myers and then Hilton—displayed a similar caprice. Valley Farm of Martin Cantine employed dozens whose families lived right in the village along with his factory workers. And the Washburn brothers joined the trend with farms run on their brickmaking profits in Flatbush, over Barclay Heights and toward Woodstock.

These farms were all pastoral retreats where their owners dabbled in, for instance, dairy because grazing cattle kept the fields open, allowing them to feel the expanse of their land. The most expansive of all these gentleman farms, with over one thousand acres right in the heart of the township, was that of James Overton Winston: Winston Farm.

The Winston Farm

The rural identity of the part of Saugerties where the Winston Farm is located was Byrnes Corners, a hamlet of small residences, boardinghouses and hotels clustered where they took advantage of the scenic panorama of the Catskill Mountains spread out over the open fields that had been there since colonial days. Today, the setting has not changed. It is the view looking west from the Thruway overpass bridge. Byrnes Corners was the crossroads community where the King's Highway met the road to Woodstock, and it ceased to exist in 1951 when the New York State Thruway removed everything to construct the pair of north and south toll plazas and maintenance area for Exit 20.

The Thruway covered not just what was Byrnes Corners but also a sizable chunk of the best of the haying fields of Saugerties Farm. The delicate balance of water, grazing and harvest feed of a dairy farm was destroyed, and the formula Saugerties Farm had famously made work for its large herds was no longer practical, just like so many other farms that the Thruway displaced by its claiming, absorbing or dividing of their land.

Saugerties Farm was the later name for the Winston Farm. J.O. Winston was an engineer. His company had been the principal contractor for constructing the dams and dikes of the Ashokan Reservoir, the Catskill water supply for New York City. This work employed hundreds of horses and mules that he had brought from his native Virginia, and his initial purchase of the Rio Alto Stock Farm in January 1912 was to buy the facilities he'd leased for wintering these animals. When he bought the adjacent Buffett lands that June, these two became the core of what would grow into what is presently the 840-plus-acre Winston Farm. He continued to add adjoining purchases and, by 1920, had consolidated the largest block of land under one title in the town of Saugerties.

What Winston found in Saugerties in the early 1910s was a lively circle of "scientific" farmers in its large estates. Edwin Cadwell, a financier from Wall Street, was experimenting with breeding Guernseys at the Shagbark Farms after buying the herds George W. Washburn had assembled there to breed stock for the many farms the Washburn family owned. Scientific agriculture was the intellectual reason for retiring to one's country seat at this time. It was the age when even the most modest estate had a greenhouse prominently placed in view of its entrance to show off this kind of pursuit.

J.O. Winston found Saugerties a place in the country where there was an understanding of his pursuits, and he found the land he had purchased perfect for an engineering approach to experiments with breeding and

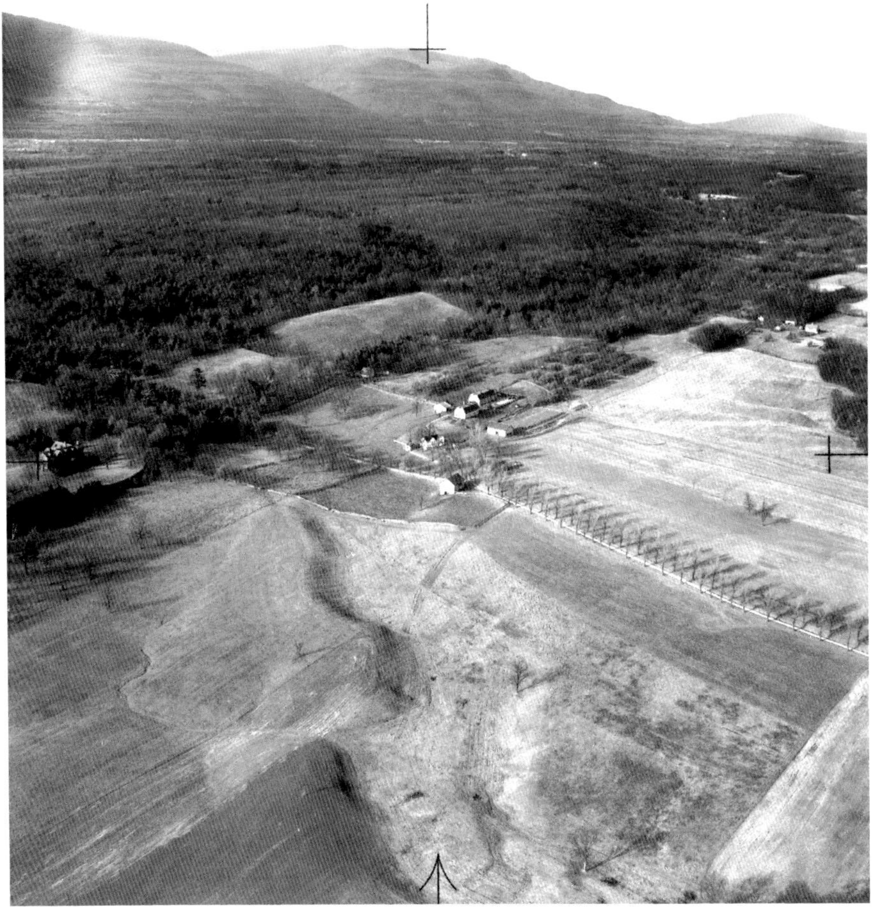

A 1955 view of the best-known open fields in Saugerties where the twenty-fifth-anniversary Woodstock Festival was held in 1994. *R&L Archive collection.*

production environments. He set up residence, and within a decade, his Guernseys were breaking records for milk production, his fowl breeding had created the capon and his trotters were major winners on the harness track circuit. Winston's farm was on the itinerary of royalty and heads of state as America's showcase for the merits of scientific agriculture for over two decades.

When Winston first took up permanent residence on the farm, he was still publishing a newspaper in Virginia and fulfilling civil engineering contracts for dams throughout the northeast. In the early 1920s, he had the nine-thousand-square-foot mansion house Kingsmead designed and built by architects Teller and Betz as his center of operations. It had a dormitory where his apprentices were housed and studios where they drew up his projects. There was a large ballroom and lounge for entertaining clients and visiting dignitaries. This house was built entirely of bluestone, and the grounds that surrounded it were landscaped with bluestone bridges, walls and dammed streams made as miniature replicas of his Ashokan reservoir. The sesquicentennial of the Revolutionary War's burning of Kingston was organized in Kingsmead in 1927.

Winston's farm is completely underlain with channels and piping for distributing the water from the natural hillside drainage to the many barns, stock pens and field troughs. At the time he purchased the property, there were many independent structures, the homes and barns of the farms he bought up, and all of these were connected to his intricate supply network. This perfectly engineered living and pasture environment and its documented effect on production and quality gave the farm an international reputation by the mid-1920s. For the next thirty years, its facilities housed large populations of tenants well before the first residential subdivisions appeared.

This land had a reputation for historic significance well before Winston's contributions. J.O. Winston's earliest purchases were within one of the first land grants in the Saugerties area—the Meales and Hayes Beaverkill part of their 1687 patent—which extends over 262 acres of rolling fields under the east face of the Hoogebergs.

This land has continually attracted owners of distinction over the centuries. The earliest was Evert Wynkoop, purported to be of the John Wincop (Johannas Wynkoop) family involved in the earliest settlement of the Hudson Valley as recipient of a 1619 land patent in the "north Virginia" for the Separatists from the Church of England. These were the Puritans who were redirected to Massachusetts.

In 1719, Evert Wynkoop purchased the middle section of the Beaverkill patent to build the first Wynkoop house here, dated to 1727. This stone house still stands and is in the national, state and local landmark registries and makes a stately introduction to Saugerties, gracing the exit view of the southbound Thruway tollbooth.

A deed of note, for land once part of the Winston Farm but now under Thruway lanes, was written to John Minqua, reputed to be the Mohawk Indian who was one of the four chiefs representing the tribal federation of New York before Queen Anne in 1710 when land was promised to the Palatines in their Schoharie territory. There is an actual document and a reference to the person and location, and it is one of the few such designations of property rights to a Native American, but this connection to the chief that was received by Queen Anne is unproven. There are, however, artifacts that have been unearthed throughout the Winston Farm that prove prehistoric habitation there as far back as 10,000 BC.

This land is at the merging of the long trail out of the Woodstock Valley with the ancient Lenne Lenape route between the Delaware basin and the Mohawk Valley. Some of the earliest European settlement can be found along these footpaths. By 1705, they had become wagon roads and highways. As the King's Highway, this was the most traveled road between the colonies. Its terminus at Albany made that location the traditional place where all Indian treaties were negotiated. There is scarcely a name in American history that did not pass this place in colonial times and during and after the Revolution.

J.O. Winston suffered losses during the Great Depression, and his son, Randolph, recovered the farm in a bankruptcy sale and incorporated it as Saugerties Farm. It functioned as a highly productive dairy farm up to the late 1940s and the arrival of the Thruway. The majority of the land was kept intact through periods of speculation in placing a country club, a golf course, a community college, a resource recovery facility and a casino, all uses based on its latter twentieth-century identity as a large tract with an interstate highway interchange right at the front door.

Kingsmead was sectioned off with one hundred acres to become a country club in the early 1950s, and Robert Trent Jones, a world-famous golf course designer, bought the remaining seven hundred acres in 1956. But all the land had returned to Winston in foreclosures by the late '50s. Having sold all the dairy herds and milk processing equipment, the land was sold for a fraction of its previous value in 1963. Afterward, local farmers religiously hayed its fields every season to keep it from overgrowing.

In 1969, after several Sound-Out performances on a small farm on the Glasco Turnpike, a similar event was attempted for the larger fields of the Winston Farm. A negative reaction sent this to a less relevant location, and the event that took place there became the famous Woodstock Festival. For that event's twenty-fifth anniversary, in 1994, the Winston Farm was represented as a permanent concert venue and was given a permit for this concert, primarily because this solidified a position in opposition to the Winston Farm's selection as a county dump site. The event attracted 350,000 attendees over a three-day weekend, but after the dump threat disappeared, the fund for supporting the permanent concert venue was applied to a building fund for a government facility and the concert venue idea faded.

The nine-thousand-square-foot Winston mansion house designed by architects Teller and Betz around elements of an original Wynkoop bluestone house is listed by the New York State Department of Parks, Recreation and Historic Preservation as a structure of historic and architectural significance and eligible for National Register designation. The overall farm has one of the last remaining roads consistently represented on maps, from the earliest, that has never been improved for the automobile. This road is used as an address for grave sites listed by the United States Department of the Interior for officers of the Revolutionary War, and the whole Winston Farm is listed as archaeologically sensitive for the many artifacts of Native American significance located there.

The Winston Farm is one of the great conundrums of Saugerties. Despite its overwhelming presence as a culturally significant place, there has never been the will to officially recognize the fact. The same thing happened with *Opus 40* with the suggestion that it be maintained as a public park. The lighthouse went through the same dismissal when, in the late 1960s, it was offered to the community by the federal government after decommissioning. The mystery is not so much that the responsibility goes unrecognized by decision makers as it is that the benefit to the community is so obvious to the community at the same time those who volunteer to take the responsibility on are so officially taken for granted.

6
A CLOSER LOOK AT AN ICON

The last great house to be built in nineteenth-century Ury was Clovelea. As a landmark of an era, an icon, a brand, Clovelea represents the essence of everything that Saugerties ever was or will ever want to be.

From the age of five, William R. Sheffield lived in Ury. He had all the advantages of the wide-open views of the whole Hudson and the entire Catskill range from his father's house, Brightbank. In 1876, he bought the land in the foreground of that property's shared view of the mountains and then spent years creating the setting where he would eventually put his own house. He first had a fine architect, Joshua Cleveland Cady, create a gatehouse and carriage house design to blend into Ury's environment. Then, after sculpting the embankments and planting the land, he had another architect who also worked in the environmentally considerate theme, Alfred H. Thorp, design his house.

So among the homages to classical monuments of half a century before that echoed Trinity Church's man-over-nature theme that heralded the coming of the industrial age, he built a house meant to echo the flow of the mountains and river and man's work of hands, to honor an appreciation of nature, which would foreshadow, or maybe even inspire, the Arts and Crafts colonies in Woodstock twenty years into the future.

This passion began when Thorp and Edward Tuckerman Potter repaired Trinity Church after a fire in 1873. As part of this work, Potter acquired a stained-glass window from Arts and Crafts master William Morris that was installed in 1874. An account of Morris showing paintings he had done of the

Saugerties landscape that year was published in *The Pearl* in 1875. No English artist would come to America without experiencing and painting the landscape that inspired the great Hudson River School of painting. This window, and Morris's presence in Saugerties, represented a moment in art history.

Since the time the earliest of the curious arrived to see the industrialization of Saugerties, artists were also attracted. The events of the 1830s in Saugerties coincided with the birth of the Hudson River School of painters. The history of Ury's involvement with the masters of this movement stretches from Thomas Cole, the founder of the movement, to Thomas Cole's son's tenure, to well past the turn of the century, as rector of Trinity Church in Saugerties. In the ending decades of the nineteenth century, it was Saugerties' relationship to Trinity Church's masterwork and the majestic views from Ury's tradition-encrusted estates that created the aura of attractiveness that would have the whole town known as a resort for decades into the twentieth century.

The romantic spirit of Ury and the picturesque views there of the river and mountains needed a patron like W. R. Sheffield and the architectural design of Alfred H. Thorp's Clovelea to punctuate that aspect of Saugerties' identity. It needed a presence not just designed to enhance Ury's environment; it needed one that expressed the joy that comes from appreciating it. This is what the art of the architect was able to create in Clovelea. William Richards Sheffield captured the spirit of a unique cultural period in Saugerties that, for half a century to follow, resounded throughout the entire region.

Prior to 1850, the prevalent architectural style in the growing village of Saugerties was the Federal and Greek Revival. After 1850, there was a strong resurgence of pride in the colonial community's Dutch heritage, and many examples of a pedestrian Dutch-style architecture worked their way into the built environment. This is evidenced in the stepped parapets of the gabled ends of structures that are dated to this period. So Saugerties already had an ample northern European influence when architects began designing structures in the later part of the 1800s, such as the gatehouse and carriage house (1878) and mansion house (1882) of Clovelea.

In the last quarter of the nineteenth century, tourism among the new social elite created an awareness of the architectural revivals in Europe, especially in the northern countries of Belgium and the Netherlands, where a culture was shared with New York City and the Hudson Valley's Dutch heritage. This resulted in a stylistic trend toward the neo-Gothic that became popular as the core of the Flemish Gothic or Flemish Modern architectural style of townhouses built in the 1880s and '90s for the affluent new districts of upper Manhattan and Brooklyn. For his Clovelea, an estate house in a Hudson

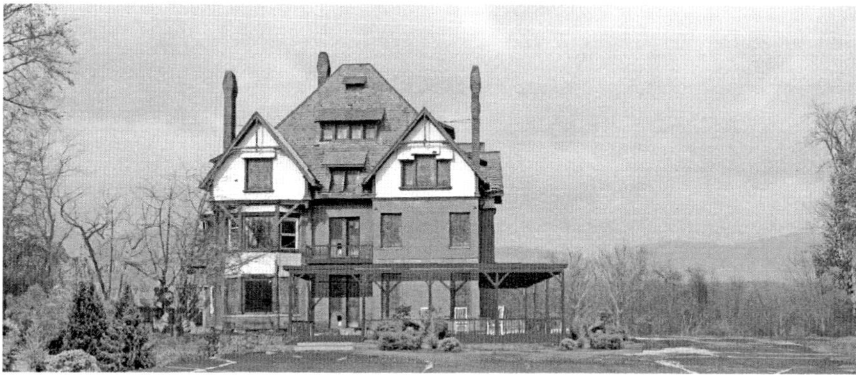

A digital sketch of a restored Clovelea mansion by the architect-owner and restorer of Clovelea's Joshua Cleveland Cady–designed carriage house. *Courtesy Scott Harrison.*

Valley community priding itself on this Dutch heritage, Sheffield selected this acceptable fashionable style of architecture.

This stylistic preference was much more in the spirit of Barclay Heights, where Clovelea is located, due to the influence of Arts and Crafts master William Morris's Trinity Church stained-glass window and its pictorial motifs created by the pre-Raphaelite masters Edward Burne-Jones, Ford Maddox Brown and William Morris himself. It represented one of the earliest examples of that movement to appear on this side of the Atlantic. The acquisition of the Morris studio work by the architectural firm of Edward Tuckerman Potter, where Alfred H. Thorp was partner, was well known to New York's cultured community of the time. When Thorp was commissioned as the architect for Clovelea's mansion house, the Medieval Revival theme in this pre-Raphaelite work was the reason. The growing trend toward the Gothic forms in the cutting edge of architecture fit the ambitious William R. Sheffield's romantic personality.

The medieval artistic influences stressed in the Arts and Crafts movement's ideals, without question, led to the turn-of-the-century creation of the artist colony of Byrdcliffe in Woodstock. Seven decades before, in the 1830s, it was the panorama of the Catskills from Saugerties' Barclay Heights that was the gateway view to artists and lovers of nature in the earliest days of the Hudson River School of painters. The architectural style chosen for the mansion house at Clovelea communicated an equal appreciation of art and nature that W. R. Sheffield intended to communicate as he framed this setting.

William R. Sheffield had spent years planning his estate's landscaping, planting the grounds as a park setting to prepare a location for the perfect positioning and scaling of a home that fit into the view it commanded. His two earliest structures—the gatehouse and the carriage house—were placed within this planning scheme as picturesque elements. They were pre-built years before to introduce a concept that would dominate the mansion house theme. Sheffield saw this theme as the overall soaring form and towering pyramidal roof, popular in this time, that formed an homage to the grandeur of the mountain escarpment's distant scenery it announced.

This view had been famous as a subject of artistic works for over fifty years when W. R. Sheffield chose it for this setting. He was well aware of the value of the scenic. Growing up at Brightbank—the original estate setting of Henry Barclay that his father, Joseph Benjamin Sheffield, purchased in 1858—his ideals were honed by one of the best views up and down the Hudson anywhere.

In 1882, the year Clovelea was built, William R. Sheffield was setting out to make a mark on Saugerties that would establish his personality as forward looking, ambitious and sensitive to his times. From the base of his ownership in the J.B. Sheffield & Son Paper Company after his father's death in 1879, he expanded to where he controlled the paper product from the processing of the pulp to the bound book and succeeded in reinvigorating Saugerties' renown as a center of innovation. In a building spurt that began after the original Barclay paper mill buildings were destroyed by fire in 1873, he acquired the Ulster Iron Works and completely rebuilt them into the pulp plant and filled the shoreline beside the paper mill with an array of new buildings, by 1888 finishing off with an office entry flanked by the massive

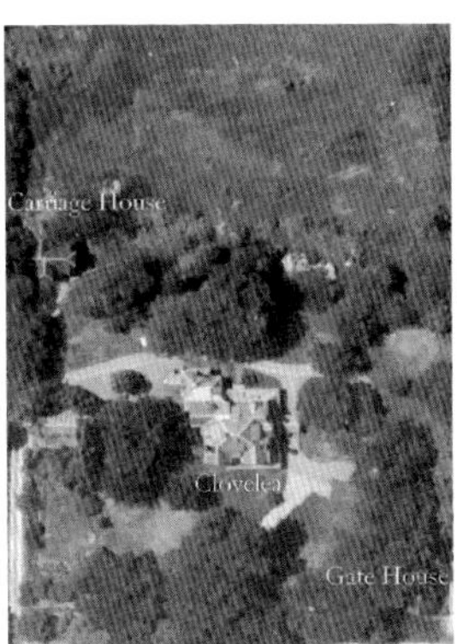

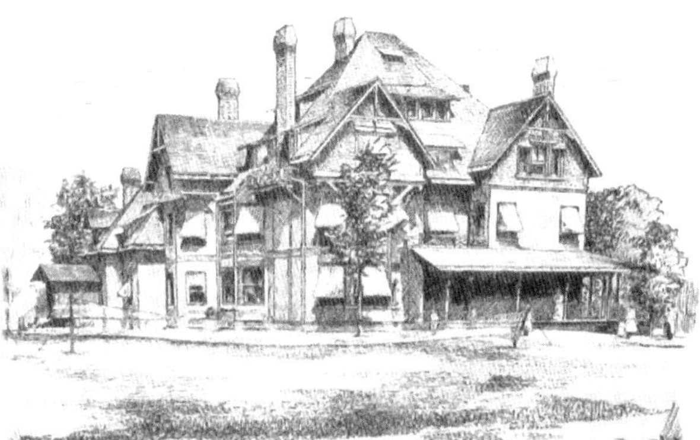

1889 sketch of the mansion of W.R. Sheffield and an aerial view from 1949 showing the plan of Clovelea. *From the author's collection.*

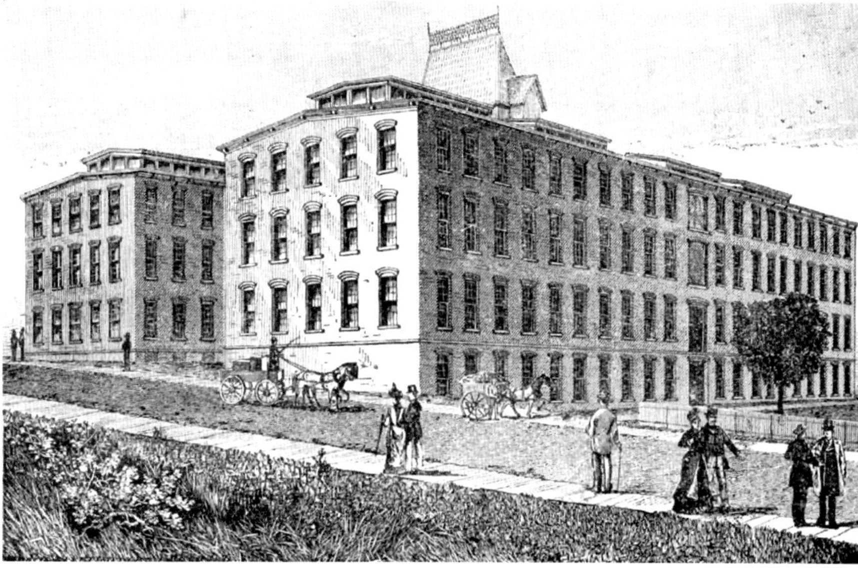

The only remaining mill structure of the Sheffield & Son Paper Company complex is the Saugerties Manufacturing Company bindery built in 1888. *Courtesy Audrey Klinkenberg.*

blank book manufacturing plant he built facing East Bridge Street. The office building, designed in the Dutch style with a massive medieval-influenced fireplace in its entry hall, was W. R. Sheffield's public space where his business ambitions could leave as much a lasting impression as his cultural ambitions left at Clovelea. But it is clear from the engravings and photographic images he used to represent what he'd built that there was a pride in their design or arrangement that went far beyond mere functionality.

W.R. Sheffield was a man of his times. His business partnership with his father and his later enterprise partnerships were secondary to his personal ambitions. He was a major influence in Republican politics locally from 1875 and in New York City after 1890. He served as president of the village of Saugerties and was on the boards of numerous banks and organizations here. After his relinquishment of the management of his companies in 1890, he chose to spend most of the remainder of his business life, right up until his death in 1913, as an agent and representative using his own personality and reputation and social and political connections on behalf of the paper industry.

The Sheffield estate retained ownership of the land under all the mills of Saugerties well into the twentieth century. However, Clovelea, the only house that Sheffield ever built, was sold a mere dozen years after it was

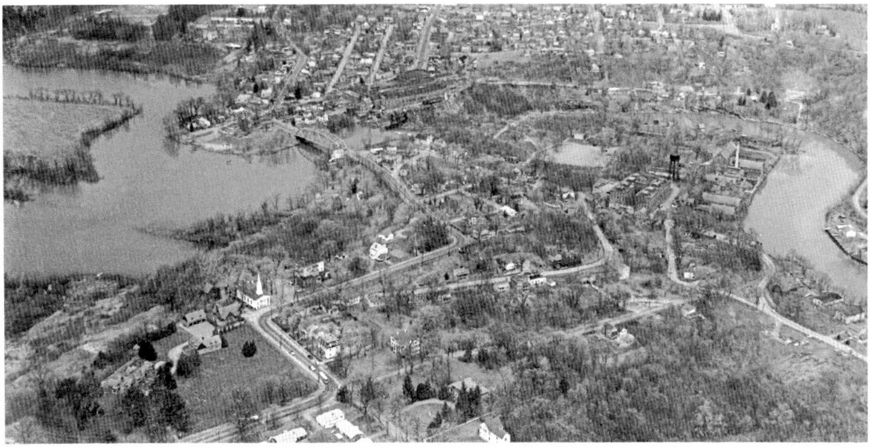

The gateway to Saugerties, past the gatehouse of Clovelea, along the streets down to the mills, as experienced in the early 1960s. *R&L Archive collection.*

finished. It was purchased by Edward Rising in 1894, when the Sheffield family began to branch out into other involvements and left Saugerties. Rising, a chemical company executive whose main residence was in New York City, purchased it for entertaining in the country following the Gilded Age trend that saw all the houses in Barclay Heights become seasonal residences of the New York City wealthy.

Rising took up full-time residence at Clovelea after retirement and died there in 1917. Clovelea was then occupied by his wife, Harriet Rising, until she died and then by their daughter Margaret until she became too old. During these sixty-eight-plus years of Rising occupancy, Clovelea was maintained as a showpiece of the residential grandeur of Barclay Heights.

Clovelea was first applied to a commercial use as the Stonewall Hotel in the 1950s and then Anton's Restaurant in the 1960s. Subdivision of part for a motel and the separation of the gatehouse and carriage house later in the 1990s brought the present acreage on which the mansion house sits down to three and a half, but this land includes the former mansion, leaving intact control of the viewshed the house was originally designed to command.

This same viewshed is what defines the gateway of Saugerties today. Clovelea is one of the few places where a perspective from a public highway connects the grandeur of a bygone era with the town and village's scenic and picturesque character. Because of this, Clovelea's reputation as an "icon" is well founded. As long as it stands, it will be a tangible symbol of the regional identity that Saugerties has presented to the world over the years.

7
THE HISTORIC LANDSCAPE OF SAUGERTIES

What cannot be erased from the historical presence is the story of landforms, both natural and man-made. The structures of documented history, now physically gone and forgotten, leave the landforms they inhabited as evidence of man's presence. That perpetual presence is far more difficult, if not impossible, to ignore. Only the land holds the history that can make Saugerties a place.

Saugerties is on one of the widest parts of the upper Hudson River. The estuary delta of the Esopus outlet on the west lies diagonally opposite the estuary delta of the Stony Creek into Tivoli Bays to the east. This part of the river was always a busy place for harvesting the rich fisheries that these deltas nourished, from the prehistoric through colonial times. In the days of sail, it was equally busy with cargo boats that used its width to maneuver into and out of the turnpike terminals on both shores.

When Henry Barclay began his developments after 1825, it was all on the south side of the Esopus Creek delta. Barclay promoted the tidewater access of his mill sites in 1826 at a fourteen-foot drought. From the documents of merchants who used the creek's north side at the base of Mynderse Hill, and around the corner at the base of Dock Street, the Esopus had a much shallower drought, in the neighborhood of six feet. The outlet of the Esopus naturally accumulates silt in its channel and builds it up nearly to the middle of the river.

There has always been considerable silting from both the Esopus and the Stony. At Tivoli Bays, the late 1840s construction of the Hudson

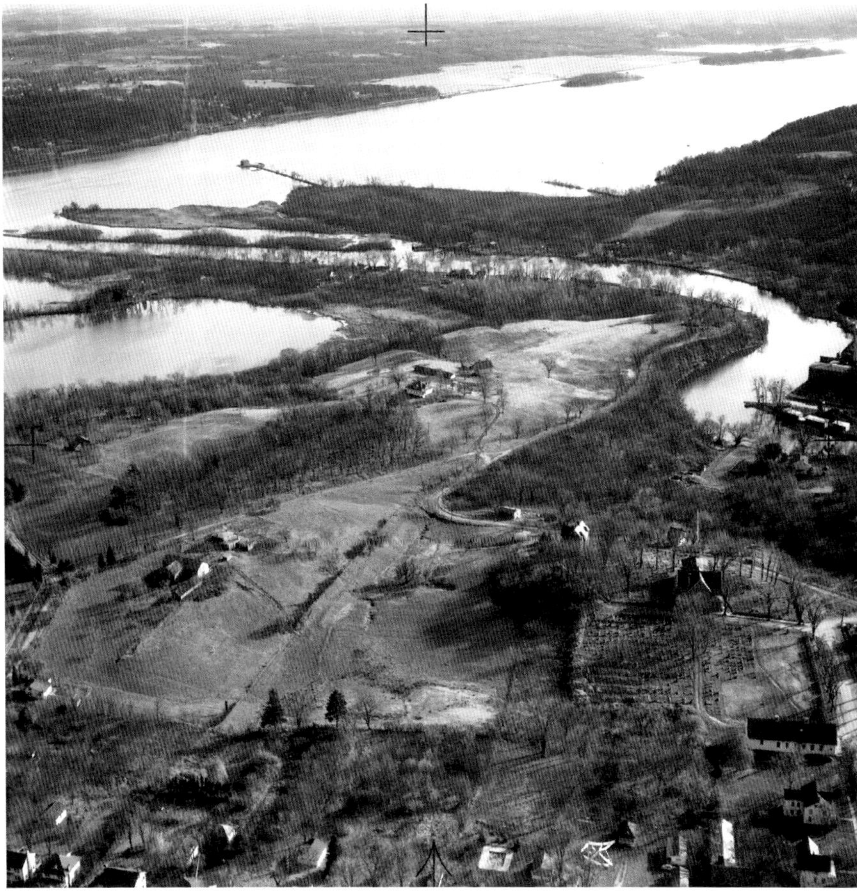

The Esopus snakes a deep cut through to the shoals and dredged navigation channel, with Tivoli's long-filled North Bay shown downriver. *R&L Archive collection.*

River Railroad bulwarks across the bays cut off the direct outlet of the Stony Creek, and the silt filled the deep water of North Bay in less than a decade.

However, the forming of the estuary at the outlet of the Esopus has a much more dramatic story, and this goes back thousands of years. This is really the story that begins the history of Saugerties.

The Esopus Shoals

An event thought to be a massive ice jam at the earliest stages of the last glacial period caused the Hudson River above Kingston to inundate the land to the 220-foot level and freeze solid. When the lead tongue of the great glacier met the valley from the northeast, it slid right over the more ancient landforms protected by this frozen lake.

As the great weight of the glacier made heat from its pressure, this frozen lake experienced an early melt that made flumes through the more ancient geology at its base. Its waters eroded outlet tunnels downward along the deep channel of the river bottom and exited out to form a broad delta on an exposed continental shelf.

One of that sunken river's tributary channels etched a groove into a vein of soft limestone running parallel to the river at Kingston. During the height of the glacier's impact, for thousands of years, this gouged ever deeper to reach an exit at Saugerties into the Hudson's channel.

When the glacier had receded, the course of this exposed gorge ran parallel to a long outcrop of rock that formed a barrier wall separating a massive lake filled with the waters of all the streams of the eastern face of the Catskill Mountains. The only thing that separated this lake from the gorge was the same limestone that had been etching away and weakening for eons.

Within recent geological time, that limestone gave way from the pressure of the lake and collapsed at the Glenerie falls. In a great flood, all the water of this lake cascaded into the small stream at the base of the deep gorge with such a force that the rock lining the steep walls above were dislodged and propelled with increasingly greater force against downstream walls until a massive debris flow moved with such momentum it was all propelled a mile out into the broad depths of the Hudson's channel. This filled the river completely for miles, even scouring a cliff face into the opposite shore. It made such a dense mass that not even the great current of the Hudson has been able to remove it to this day.

This debris field is the Esopus Shoals. Today, the Saugerties lighthouse stands on the edge of these shoals where they end abruptly at the depths of the Hudson River's shipping channel. Standing on the lighthouse's base, you look over one of Hudson River Valley's most prominent features. The lighthouse and the equally evocative landform of the Long Dock mark this as both a natural and cultural marvel.

Henry Hudson had to pilot the *Half Moon* to exactly where the Saugerties lighthouse is positioned in the channel of the Hudson River because the deep channel has always been pinched over a mile east from the Esopus's outlet on the western shore.

There is little doubt that the first Europeans to get the first long view of the great continent of America got it from almost exactly where the Saugerties lighthouse sits today.

The lighthouse is constructed on a crib of stone whose surface is roughly the height above the water of the *Half Moon*'s mid-deck. The tower's lamp room is the height of the lookout on the *Half Moon*'s main mast. So in September 1609, the first group of people ever to be inspired with a vision of an American future began that by examining the western horizon seen from this place as they contemplated the face of the Catskill Mountains in the ebb and flow of a river that experienced the struggle of forces that converged here eons ago when the Esopus first became assimilated into the Hudson.

Here, friendly souls came out from deep back in the Esopus's stream to greet them, carrying in their canoes gifts. They also brought the cascade of insight into the potential of the land that motivated Hudson to survey and log the resources of this place, reinforcing the memory of that first vision by identifying and enumerating it in detail.

Scattered documents from history carry the story from there on. This encounter was published and read throughout Europe. A 1618 patent to John Wyncop for settling separatists into a colony in "North Virginia" stemmed from it. That ended up the Plymouth colony. Then, in 1624, the Dutch sent shiploads of Walloons, establishing their claim to New Netherlands, and divvied everything up among the patroons.

All this started at the Esopus Shoals, but throughout this period of early settlement, these Esopus Shoals remained a barrier that deftly kept Saugerties at a distance from it all. The potential behind these shoals watched and waited as colonial period sloops passed bearing furs, as Revolutionary War ships anchored and blasted houses and as the early decades of the new Republic lurched by on the first steamboats.

Then, just as the celebratory barge of the newly completed Erie Canal carried water from far across the misty Catskill peaks that first impressed Hudson's mariners, the Esopus Shoals lifted its veil, and within a dozen years the first lighthouse was built to mark the nearly lost place of that moment in our race memory.

Within the single year of 1825, enough material was floated through the shoals to build and equip two factories and to construct enough housing to support a population that increased fifty-fold over the previous number of souls that settled Saugerties in the decades before.

Before 1839, when the first lighthouse was built and a channel was made deep enough to admit a steamboat, everything was rafted or ferried through the shoals from warehouses on the river's eastern shore or was carted from where channels on the west shore allowed steamboats to land at Bristol, two miles north, or Glasco, two miles to the south. By the time a passage was deepened through the Esopus Shoals, that river traffic was servicing a population of thousands.

In the decades around the turn of the century, the channel through the shoals had been deepened and widened, but the Esopus Shoals still performed its age-old purpose. It managed its environment, resisting the runaway shore-based development the river traffic brought north and south of it. By its intractable character, it forced the population to spread the transportation base inland to the railroad and to create some of the first paved automobile roads in the state. That brought the benefit of a more preserved scenic character to the waterfront than many other places. In an era when little but icehouses could be seen from the river, the shoals made this shoreline a Mecca for those who appreciated an earlier scenic quality in their destination.

Sometime around a century into its culture-forming exercise, our Esopus Shoals began a return to nature. The well-tended channel that welcomed the passenger-bearing steamboat and ferry was no longer necessary as bridges were built and the highway replaced the river. In the brief period between the opening of the Erie Canal and the opening of the Thruway, the legendary past that forms the history of Saugerties had been orchestrated under the direction of the Esopus Shoals and that task was complete.

When this all began, it was because Henry Barclay needed to have a deep-water harbor to fulfill his promise of mills adjacent tidewater in the age of water power—a rare geographic occurrence. Dredging a channel through the Esopus Shoals was one of the earliest engineering projects in his plans for the development of Saugerties.

All of Barclay's plans involved controlling water and its power. In every case, he did this with the available rock of his land, either channeling through it or cutting and building with it. The structure of the holding wall for Barclay's canal, still clearly visible, is what the mass of the diversion dam was that he built twenty feet high across the falls of the Esopus. His plans for the structures that formed the quays at the base of the mills were the same.

Today, a level area, all fill, stretches behind a stone bulkhead laid between two massive outcrops from the base of East Bridge Street to the tip of the easterly

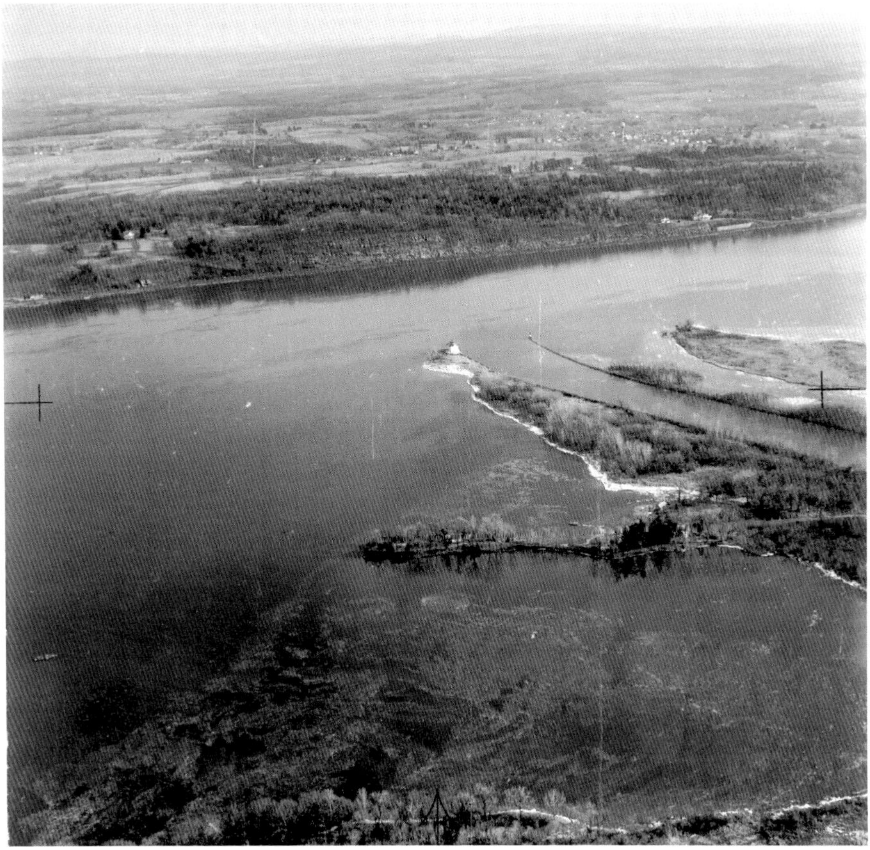

The Saugerties lighthouse lies up against the opposite bank of the river as it marks the edge of the Esopus Shoals. *R&L Archive collection.*

most solid ground. In what was once tide-filled marsh are now the dredges of the Esopus channel, where this bulkhead has raised the land to a height well above the threat of the highest tide. This wall is strategically placed on the outside curve of the flow of the Esopus's current. The depths are continually flushed there, and it is the only place where dredging is not necessary to keep the channel clear and deep. On today's river charts, this corner is marked at a depth of twenty-six feet thanks to that continuous scouring.

The general lay of the land indicates that the site of the quarrying of these building stones for the bulkheads is at the base of East Bridge Street. Some cutting at the outcrop there is still clearly visible. That formation likely stretched out to more than twice what remains there today and may have been substantially higher.

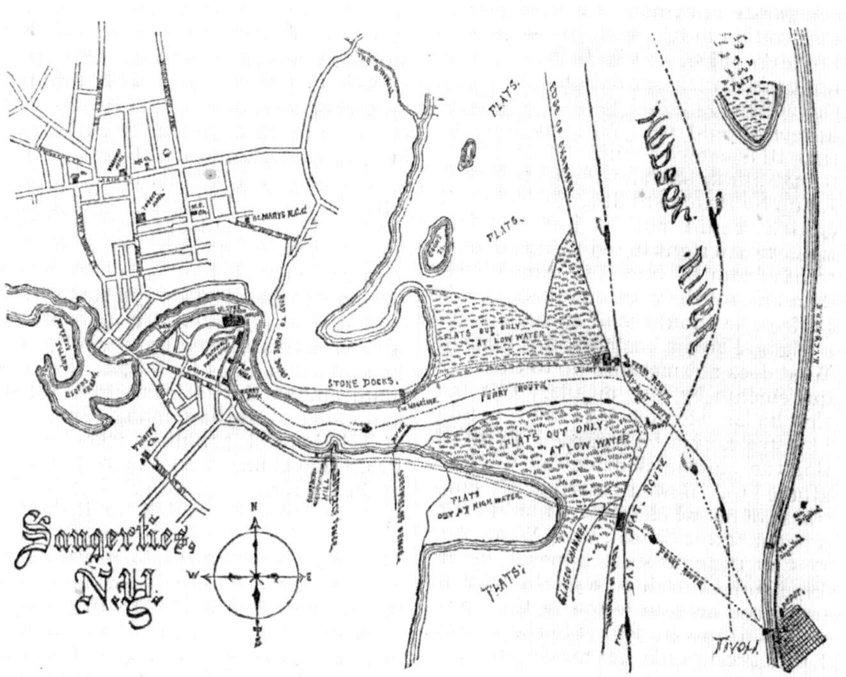

Map in the December 9, 1875 *Kingston Freeman* illustrating an article about creating a long dock north or south of the Esopus. *Courtesy Audrey Klinkenberg.*

Henry Barclay originally planned storehouses and shipbuilding operations on this filled marsh. In 1826, he was promoting an ideal location for shipbuilding at the same time his paper and iron mills were being built. This would have made the entire south shore of the Esopus channel out to the channel of the Hudson lined with ships under construction, utilizing, as he wrote, sawmills and the manufacture of iron fittings directly on site.

This did not happen, but in 1875, Leon Barritt, Saugerties' most imaginative citizen of the time, stepped out into the shoals and did soundings all the way to the middle of the river across what was called Schoonmaker Flats and suggested that Ferry Street could be extended out to the Hudson Channel in line with the Saugerties lighthouse. He created a map, interviewed all the parties with an interest in commerce and published his proposal for building a pier and depot as the next generation of riverfront improvements to Saugerties. That eventually led to the Saugerties Pier Bill in the New York legislature and the 1876 construction of the Long Dock under the Saugerties Long Dock and Improvement Company.

THE LONG DOCK

Today, Ferry Street in the village extends to the edge of Schoonmaker's Flats, which is part of the original Henry Barclay lands, and enters the town to continue on to the middle of the river across the jetty sanctioned by the state under the Pier Act. A ferry depot and ferry slip are at the terminus. This extension of Ferry Street is the Long Dock.

The Long Dock and Ferry Depot, along with the Saugerties lighthouse and the buildup of the dredging spoils from 150 years of continuous use of the shipping channel to Saugerties' mills, altogether today highlight the Esopus Shoals as the most visually distinctive man-made element of any map that can be found.

By 1877 and '78, the Long Dock had made Saugerties a major transit center for rail-based cargo and passengers ferried to and from Tivoli. It also offered quick transfer of passengers and cargo from river steamboats. It made Saugerties' coaches more competitive than Kingston and Catskill transportation for carrying vacationers to the great mountain houses and forced development of rail lines into the mountains at each. The Long Dock was essentially the beginning of Saugerties' visibility as a tourist destination and gateway community.

At the same time the Long Dock was opening for business, John and James Kiersted were opening their newly rebuilt Overlook Mountain House on the mountain closest to, and clearly visible from, the Saugerties' Long Dock depot.

With the construction of the Long Dock, storehouses began to populate the south shoreline of the Esopus. Whereas, up to this point, Saugerties harbor had been limited to traffic related to the mills that shipped out manufactured products, with more rapid transfers from the Long Dock, freight forwarding became an everyday part of the Saugerties' economy, and improvements in streets and hotels to accommodate the new traffic followed.

Materials by ferry and steamboat to Saugerties had quicker access to the inland markets, and this in turn sparked new ventures in the village, such as insurance and banking, that supported the small businesses that thrived on low shipping costs and quick access to markets. It is this level of business that set the mercantile theme in the documentation for Saugerties' Main and Partition Streets National Register Historic District.

The Long Dock's impact on Saugerties begins with the referee sale of the public/private Saugerties Long Dock and Improvement Co. after the Town of Saugerties refused to financially support its construction. W.R.

Sheffield, J.W. Davis, Henry Turck and G.R. Spaulding, the board of the company, bought it and then owned it privately as the Saugerties Long Dock Company.

Numerous newspaper articles of the period follow this progression of events and make a good study of the contrast between progressive, entrepreneurial post–Civil War thinking and that of more conservative business interests. The key protagonist, William R. Renwick, the owner of the steamboat *Ansonia* with its exclusive docking arrangements at the wharves of his Ulster White Lead Company, had the most to lose from every boat on the river stopping at the Long Dock.

With the Long Dock, the wharves of Saugerties that had been built to attract shipbuilding and had grown into a support function for the mills now were a major benefit to the business enterprises of the larger region, including the resorts and boardinghouses of the countryside. In 1851, when the Hudson River Railroad came to Tivoli, ferries that brought steamboat passengers and cargo from the warehouses there returned to the importance they held before dikes and navigation aids made Saugerties Harbor a home port for its own steamboats. When the Long Dock was finished in 1877 to shorten the ferry distance to the Tivoli trains and support a direct stop for steamboats, it again made Saugerties a focus of the transportation routes of the day.

By 1881, the West Shore Railroad had opened operations in Saugerties, and its harbor became busy forwarding freight across the river to the rail routes going east into New England. It wasn't until well after the 1889 Poughkeepsie Railroad Bridge made direct cross-river railroad passage possible that this advantage began to be eliminated and the Long Dock decline in economic importance.

After the railroad, steamboats in general were used less for freight, and new storehouses in Saugerties began to be built at the tracks on the village's newly annexed west side, over a mile from the river. Even William R. Renwick found it more practical to ship white lead from the Mount Marion West Shore freight depot and lost interest in harassing the Long Dock Company. After the West Shore Railroad arrived, he sold his Saugerties Transportation Company and steamboat *Ansonia* to Robert A. Snyder, who made the company the Saugerties and New York Steamboat Company.

The waterfront kept its importance as the center of transportation in Saugerties for a while. The river continued to represent the more comfortable way to travel, and Saugerties continued to be an attractive destination for vacationing travelers preferring riverboats. But its scenic approach to the inner harbor was more appealing than being dropped off in the middle of the river, and the Long Dock became less and less used. Within twenty years of its construction, it fell into disuse, and wharf structures built based on its business followed it in decline.

Aside from the tidewater structures that changed whole shorelines, the most enduring impression from man-made landforms in Saugerties is found in the water power earthworks: the dams, reservoirs, millpond, canals, raceways and flumes. This was all the primary investment of Henry Barclay.

Barclay's Canal

Henry Barclay owned all the rights to the Esopus Creek from where the high tide mark of Hudson River waters belong to the people of New York State to the forty-six-plus-foot flood line the dam of his millpond raised the water of the creek above this tide. Every drop of this water was planned into a power system that could drive the industry he brought to Saugerties in 1825.

For nearly two centuries, deeds that originated from Henry Barclay's time have carried in them rights for using this water. They memorialize a running tally of the ways this power was used in the earliest decades of the Early Industrial Revolution in America. The engineering requirements, the manufacturing processes and every equipment specification for water power in these deeds traces a historic standard for this most valuable asset of a nineteenth-century industrial site.

The importance of Barclay's millpond's bedrock base as it continued through the rock cut and canal no. 1 was explicit in every level of deed, contract, agreement and every record of professional discourse. The canal tapped the bottom of the pond, and every bit of that water pressure was calculated in the energy it produced. Property values for these early industrial sites were based on those water rights and not only the calculations of the amount of water but also the horsepower rating of the mill wheels it drove. By the last years of the nineteenth century, this measure had reached a state of science where calculations of the ecology of the entire Catskill Mountains' eastern front was broken down into the equations of these legal instruments.

By this time, at the end of the nineteenth century, water power was entering a new era of use. The great asset in the deed to the land now called Cantine's Island—its right to first use of the water power—was no longer used since the

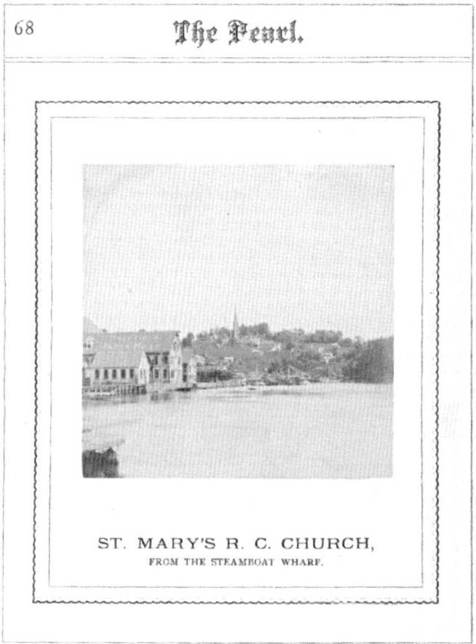

By 1875, the paper mill and spire of St. Mary's Catholic Church had introduced Saugerties to steamboat travelers for nearly four decades. *Courtesy Audrey Klinkenberg.*

iron works and its successor, the pulp mill, had not operated for a decade. In a 1903 agreement, that right was transferred to the north side of Barclay's dam, which was formerly excluded from the earlier rights to use the water. This extinguished the rights the old Ulster Iron Works property had been famous for since 1826.

The story of creating water power in Saugerties should be embedded in the imagination of every schoolchild of Saugerties. It began in the year 1825, in early fall. Men were clearing trees down to the stumps and earth down to bedrock behind the cliff seen today from the bridge. The workers are nameless, but the guess is they were the same Scots-Irish who had most recently worked on the Erie Canal. In a surviving ledger book of Henry Barclay are listed the accounts of names like Bolton and Wurts and others associated with the management of that work. The same names would be found a year later constructing the great Delaware and Hudson coal canal.

The job Henry Barclay planned was to cut blocks of stone the size of steamer trunks from this wall of solid rock to take down seventy feet in a twenty-foot-wide slice, hundreds of feet long, and form a level extension of the bedrock base of the Esopus Creek through the base of a canal, continuing to cut more blocks of stone at this lowest level of the canal base for a large flat shelf twenty feet above sea level, creating the bed for a reservoir.

These blocks of stone were finished into the material to build two massive stone dams. The first was for containing the reservoir on the leveled shelf area cut into the back side of the ridge. The second would dam the Esopus Creek and divert its water through the canal into the reservoir.

Henry Barclay's plan was to put all the water pressure of the Esopus Creek into the reservoir and use it to power the huge water wheels of an iron mill's hammers and rollers and also a paper mill's machinery. He was engineering a generator to power a mill complex. This was a radical idea in 1825.

Maps from the early 1850s show the layout of this power system. Contracts and deeds describe the water power and the water wheels and buildings that were being installed and constructed at the same time as these waterworks. That system was to work as soon as the water was harnessed. This was a grand experiment in production development.

Of that early system detailed on those early maps, there is today only the rock cut seen from the bridge and the corner of the reservoir wall at the parking lot of the Mill. These are the only clues to a story in which an experienced foreman from the Erie Canal measured the height of the land and calculated all the earth that had to be moved; the rock cut was sliced by men down to the bed level of the Esopus above its rapids over the winter; the first flood passed water through this cut in the spring; this nascent engineer was able to measure up the new work year by calculating what the reservoir could hold; the blocks sliced from the rock cut were used to build up the corner where the two arms of the reservoir meet, capping this lowest point in the direction of those first spring floods to ever touch that side of the great rock formation that for eons had diverted the flow of the Esopus but where now they are allowed to seep incessantly through to this very day.

Those walls that began to be built out from this corner eventually reached a height of twenty feet. When this was done, everything quarried from the reservoir's bed was carried through the rock cut to build the twenty-foot-high stone wall across the Esopus. By the time both stone walls were complete, it would have been the fall of 1826 and the calculated volume of an average fourteen-foot-deep pond in the Esopus and at this reservoir held back by these dams was ready to supply power at an elevation of twenty feet above two mill sites that were already constructed and equipped with machines.

The incredible amount of planning and labor that went into filling this reservoir is today lost in the landscape changes it made, now overgrown by trees. But in 1826, it was a powerful, shiny new attraction for everyone wanting to see what the industrial future looked like. The word got out, and spectators arrived to watch every advance of the workers right up to that first filling with the Esopus Creek's waters.

This was the beginning of Saugerties. Shortly after water first flowed through the rock cut, a population of hundreds began busily building the walls, roofs and docks of more mills and then an entire village. The builders of the waterworks moved on, but factory workers, their families and all the merchants of a village to feed, outfit and entertain rapidly replaced them. For the next hundred years, the story of these first builders was such a part of the life of this new village that they remained in its common memory.

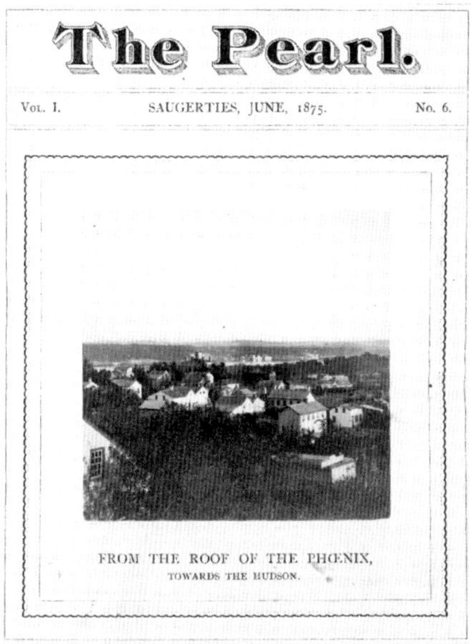

The Pearl.

Vol. I. SAUGERTIES, JUNE, 1875. No. 6.

FROM THE ROOF OF THE PHŒNIX, TOWARDS THE HUDSON.

The 1875 village center held views of its lifeblood in the harbor and across the river at the railroad terminal of Tivoli. *Courtesy Audrey Klinkenberg.*

There was an appreciation of the Herculean work that created a power source that became all the work done by every generation in Saugerties over that century.

But as with the Long Dock, this too was to trace the end of an era. At the height of Saugerties' water power–based industry, the entire shoreline from the dam to the steamboat wharves was one continuous mill complex where every process used in the manufacture of paper products, from raw material to end product, was represented in their order of manufacture. The iron works that had seen its day was replaced by the Barclay Fibre Company mill that used the brand-new process of converting wood to paper pulp. Next in line was the Sheffield Paper Company that used a percentage of this wood pulp together with its traditional rag pulp in the machines that produced rolls of paper using the same process Henry Barclay introduced in America for the first time in 1827. Then a portion of the Sheffield mill's production went up to the newest building, the Saugerties Manufacturing Company, to become bound books and envelopes.

It is the position of this bindery, built up East Bridge Street without its own wharf, that most represents a change that would affect everything. It was built after steam began to be the principal power source for manufacturing and after the West Shore Railroad began operations. The transportation benefit of being on tidewater didn't matter anymore, and Kingston, as a rail hub, had overtaken Saugerties as a manufacturing center.

Within a few decades, the water power benefits of the Esopus in Saugerties would also be subverted. By 1903, the bindery was still using water power, but the Cantine Mill, built at the same time, had begun using its water rights to generate electricity for running its machinery.

So it can be said that the advantages of Saugerties' water resources became history with the building of the bindery in 1888.

Visions of accomplishing the impossible that were exemplified by Saugerties are presently diluted by easy fantasies, but in this earlier time there was ample activity, and there is still today, accessible on the water to keep that excitement alive. Malden-on-Hudson, or Bristol with its Bristol Turnpike and deep water of the Bristol Channel, is historically where this was always most easily accessed.

The Bristol Channel

The deep channel of the Hudson crosses it diagonally after hugging the east bank past the Esopus Shoals at the Saugerties lighthouse and then touches the opposite, west side of the river at Malden. It is over fifty feet deep right against the shore there and remains this depth past Bristol Beach, Eaves Point and Wanton Island in a straight run called the Malden-on-Hudson Reach. Past this reach, the river bends eastward in a course that takes it up to ten miles' additional travel away from the Catskill front and the interior.

Half a dozen or more historical landings supported this freighting channel's closest point to the continental plateau. The landings along this shoreline of Saugerties were the most efficient access point to the continent's commerce during the age of early overland transportation by turnpikes. In the age of Saugerties' renown, this was the place of dreams and visions where ships that crossed the oceans sailed and steamed past and stopped.

As a vast variety of enterprises blossomed in the interior, in the mountains and beyond, deep draft vessels increasingly relied on the warehouses, wharf facilities and overland coaches and teamsters along the Bristol Channel for their transfer and business transactions. This prominence continued as nineteenth-century tourism and summer resorts took hold even as overland modes of transportation changed.

Malden was the most active of these ports. It was founded in 1812 to take advantage of this close relationship between the river and the mountains. Its name was later changed from Bristol to be a post office address when Bristol was found to be already taken. Bristol, though, still remains the name for the shipping channel. Today a street, River Road, runs along what was once its wharves. Some of their forms can still be seen at low tide. Many original stores and offices, now residences, can still be identified there, too. Up the inclines, many original houses have been maintained in their nineteenth-century condition.

North along the channel, Eaves Point Road allows access to an original landing feature. Here, you can picnic right next to the deep channel. Between Malden and Eaves Point is Bristol Bay and Bristol Beach, an undeveloped State Park. All of this shoreline is accessed from the water via a boat launching site at the extreme north end of Malden's River Road.

Starting from sea level at the tidewater of the fifty-foot-deep Bristol Channel, the original Bristol Turnpike rises up to cross the farmlands of the Bristol Bluffs, passes the stone houses of colonial Kaatsbaan and climbs the foothills of the Catskills to Quarryville. It reaches the base of the mountains at Palenville in the famous Kaaterskill Clove and ascends this on its north wall to reach the two-thousand-foot elevation of the Continental Plateau at Tannersville.

Reaching the tanneries in these hemlock forests was the historic destination of this road, and the Bristol Channel is the place where that journey had always begun. Once the two-thousand-foot elevation is reached, all waters flow gently west and the land levels out into fertile valleys from central New York down into northern Pennsylvania. This was all frontier and Indian lands up to the Revolution, and that is what gave the Bristol Channel its significance in American history.

The Bristol Channel has bustled with activity since the earliest days of Saugerties history. Bristol Bay was known as Lookerman's Haven in Dutch times. Lookerman was the name of a prominent fur trader. The entire stretch became famous just after 1711 with Queen Anne's settlement of Palatines in the West Camps. The British navy's interest in the Bristol Channel brought the Crown to own all the land along this shore. It settled German Palatine refugees there for growing hemp for rope and harvesting pitch from the pine to make tar. This venture failed, and some of the refugees cut the first cross-country road from the camps to the Schoharie Valley and moved there. Others moved inland to clear adjacent forests and settle some of the earliest homesteads of Saugerties.

These Palatines mainly settled parallel to the King's Highway around Kaatsbaan. Kaatsbaan is Dutch for a kind of tennis court. A level stone platform the Native Americans used for playing ball was there, and the Palatines built a stone church on it that is still there today. The roads they created to their farmsteads formed the early east–west routes between the river and the mountains. Their frontier stone houses were structured to defend these early transportation routes, and their defensive character became the character of the community.

During the Revolutionary War, in October 1777, the whole of the Bristol Channel was filled with the British fleet, which anchored there after burning Kingston. Its principal mission was to secure this pinch point between the mountains and the navigable channel for supporting the army approaching from the north. Together with their Indian allies in the inland forests, they intended to make the northern front of the war Saugerties. Defeat at Saratoga interrupted this plan, but the threat this presented made the Palatines solidly behind the rebellion.

After the Revolution, the land-based economy of the Palatine and early Dutch settlers went through a proto-entrepreneurial stage as they created riverfront market outlets from the fortress-like points they had developed along the Bristol Channel. The many roads they had developed to access these points from their farms became associated with their different families. A number of boat building yards sprang up, and a large number of vessels were operated from these landings.

Commercial interest that related the whole of the Catskill Mountains to the Hudson River, however, wasn't a concern of these farm-to-market ventures. It took the enterprising character of Connecticut Yankees to productively develop toll roads and modern ports. In 1810, a group of such businessmen laid out Glasco and the Glasco Turnpike as a branch of the Ulster and Delaware Turnpike. This was for a more direct route to cross the Hudson and extend the road into Connecticut. In this era, every venture that formed along the river was centered on moving goods teamed in from the newly productive farms of the interior to feed the now semi-urban population of old New England. The turnpikes with the shortest routes to the Hudson River were the prime investment opportunities of the day.

Malden was founded shortly after Glasco. Asa Bigelow came from Connecticut to settle in Glasco and take advantage of the turnpike for his business plan, but he was not able to buy into the company developing it. He found after setting up business in Saugerties that the Esopus Shoals made navigating to the river too difficult, so he purchased the Godfried DeWolven patent and the VanSteenberg farm and established a village, known in 1812 as Bristol and now Malden, where the Bristol Channel first touches the western shore.

A whole bevy of Bigelow relatives soon settled in Bristol to help the business build and run its turnpike to the tanneries in the mountains. The business bought cargoes of raw hides, transported and sold them to the tanneries and then purchased them as finished hides to sell to manufacturers. From 1815 into the 1830s, tanning solidified Malden's reputation as a port.

For a brief fifteen years, entrepreneurial transporters working the turnpikes controlled the economy of Saugerties. Most of the early Palatine families supplied the long-haul teamsters for the turnpikes, and a concept of the use of roads for a livelihood was common to the general population. This instilled a belief that any growth potential had to utilize turnpike and related roads to be beneficial.

So after 1825, when the Erie Canal had cut the cost of freight from $100 a ton to $9 and long-haul turnpikes were made unprofitable, the routes within Saugerties quickly became busy supporting the construction and commerce opportunity of the new industrial population. The flurry of activity around the creation of water power and mills and setting them in production guaranteed that all ports north and south of the village of Ulster profited greatly before the deep channel and bridge for the village could be completed.

Once the innovativeness of this industrial community registered as a place for the intellectual and the curious to visit, the ports and roads into the scenic countryside became increasingly popular as destinations for artists and naturalists. Along with them came a fresh look at the potential of materials of the countryside. The idea that products from the mountains could find ready transport to the cities of the coast by the Hudson River and far inland by the Erie Canal promised great profit potential to discoveries found just a few miles inland or right on the Hudson River shoreline. By midcentury, the already established forwarding enterprises that lined the Bristol Channel had taken on new identities as centers for shipping the product of bluestone quarries, brick manufacturers and other extraction and manufacturing industries that the countryside's population suddenly found the bounty of its lands brought forth. This kept the shoreline, turnpikes and homegrown businesses in the hamlets bustling well into the early twentieth century.

With steady activity from the steamboats along the shoreline feeding the turnpikes, even in the years of the decline of local industry, summer boarders continued to keep an economy alive based on the draw of this versatile environment. The mystique of the river to mountains connection that originated with the Bristol Channel began to falter only with the coming of the railroad and then automobiles.

Now, two hundred years after the first turnpikes, rarely does anyone see the mountains in the context of arriving from the river, the only way it was possible to experience them for hundreds of years before. From the Bristol shore of Saugerties, where majestic oceangoing freighters are only yards away in its channel, a car can travel on essentially the same route that in

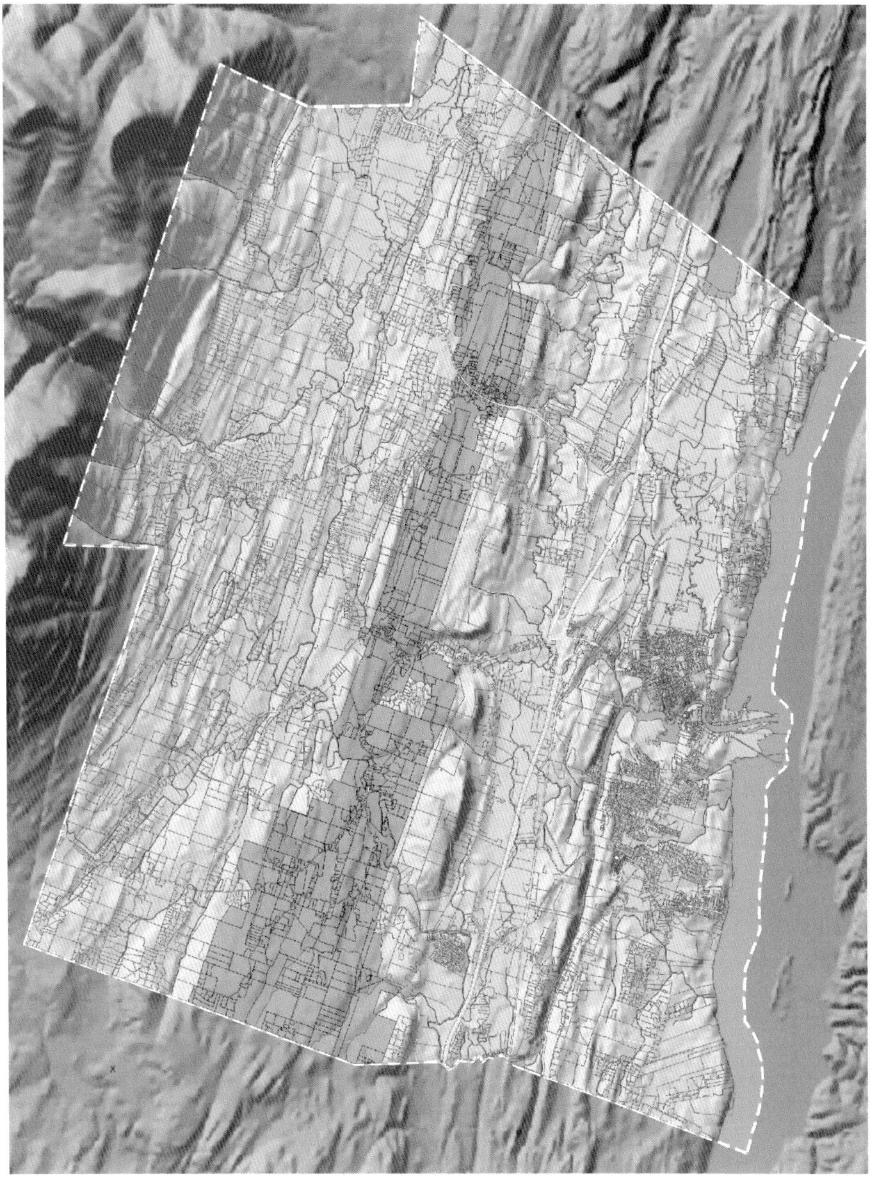

The most valuable seam of bluestone runs up the center of Saugerties where the formation's base is exposed. *Interpretive map by the author.*

1815 would have reached the same two-thousand-foot elevation and looked down on the same river, only today it would take less than half an hour. That would be the same place of departure taken by the earliest of the

Hudson River School painters, heading toward the same destination—but they usually walked.

The experience of thousands or maybe millions of dreamers and seekers of revelation from the past can be sensed in the anticipation of a destination that was just a sloop or steamboat ride from the smoky city. Fresh air and the wonders of mountain trails with long views that were the cinematic experience of the day made the idea of journeying toward a destination the draw of this shoreline for over a century. A feeling that something great is attainable from here is the impression it conveys yet today.

But this sense of a land of possibilities can actually be exponentially surpassed in one visit to a six-acre landscape made into a sculptural creation that single-handedly punctuates all the lessons of a history of the hundred years of artistic creations that came before it.

The resources most identified with Saugerties are less those of attractiveness than they are of attractions. Where the aesthetic has drawn attention to vistas renowned as the scenes of the Hudson River School of painters, those destinations were being appreciated during the same exact time when the waters and land formations pictured in these natural settings

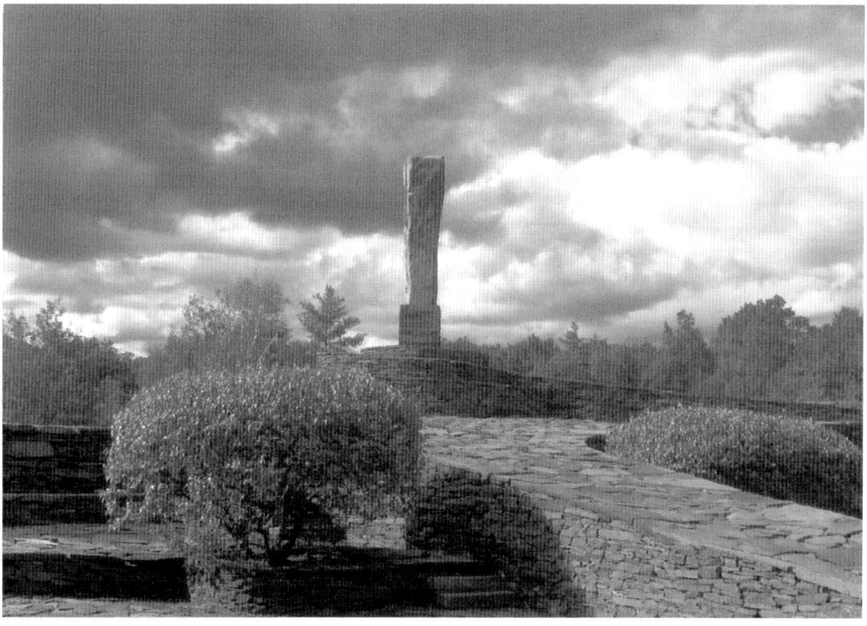

Opus 40 is a six-acre large sculpture in an early twentieth-century bluestone quarry made of the material it left behind. *Courtesy Chester Hartwell.*

were being captured and harvested as economic resources. The founder of that school of painting, Thomas Cole, would naturally prefer a less bustling place, in Catskill, for his home and studio.

The sensitivities of these seemingly polar opposite influences, however, joined as a theme later, into the twentieth century, as industrial structures began attracting artists to settings of the historic region surrounding the Woodstock art colony. Beginning with the photographs of R. Lionel De Lisser in *Picturesque Ulster* and on through the many paintings of mills, working boats and the cubist spaces of quarries from this period, Saugerties can be recognized as a favorite location for the easel and camera.

But from this period's fascination with the aesthetics of the man-made environment comes perhaps the most unique and most timeless artwork in the world: Harvey Fite's *Opus 40*.

Opus 40

Harvey Fite was born on Christmas Day 1903, in Pittsburgh, Pennsylvania, to a family with roots in Pittsburgh's hardscrabble working class. When he was still a small child, the family moved to rural Texas, where he grew up working alongside his father farming and doing carpentry. At twenty, he was accepted into the Houston Law School but left to study for the ministry at St. Stephen's College before graduating. A scholarship through his bishop made this possible.

Working with stage sets and acting at St. Stephen's drew him to the theater. In 1929, he left college to follow an acting career with the Jitney Players in Woodstock, studying and acting at the Maverick Theater. He was first attracted to sculpture there while living in the Maverick artists' colony.

By his twenty-seventh birthday, Fite realized he had, from a diary entry of December 24, 1929, "tried in vain to escape the work of hands by studying for the professional life." So in 1930, he returned to St. Stephen's to complete his degree and then resigned himself to work as a full-time wood sculptor. He spent the early Depression years producing "work of hands" as a struggling artist.

In 1933, recognized as both a theatrical designer and a dedicated sculptor, the "professional life" came to him. He was asked to head a newly founded Fine Arts Department at St. Stephen's after it became a liberal arts college affiliated with Columbia University, renamed Bard College.

Bard today has a reputation as a free-spirited school. It may be said that Fite's many years' journey of creative soul searching leading to this work of hands had more than a passing influence on the multi-disciplined seat of the arts that became Bard's identity. The initial project he undertook at Bard—directing and working alongside his students to hand-build Orient Hall, where performance, sculpture and other fine arts studies eventually grew into the college's signature Art Division—early defined Bard's independent character. Harvey Fite chaired this division until his retirement in 1969 as professor emeritus.

Harvey Fite's own identity as a sculptor began to surface with a 1935–36 sabbatical from Bard. He studied under the sculptor Corrado Vigni in Florence, after which his focus shifted from wood to stone carving. This shift led to his purchase in December 1937 of an abandoned bluestone quarry as a source of stone for this new medium. During the winter of the next year, with a Carnegie Institute Fellowship, he traveled to the Mayan archaeological site in Copan, Honduras, to study and restore Mayan sculpture. Upon his return, he commenced construction of a studio home at the site of his bluestone quarry, setting in motion the course that would ultimately lead to *Opus 40*.

From his experience in Copan, we can imagine Harvey Fite first envisioning *Opus 40* from his abandoned quarry–facing home as if the rubble piles there were ancient creations—in ruin. As in Copan's ruined complex of structures, he would have imagined a monumental earthwork and formalized that rubble landscape into ideal positions for display or performance. That would have been Harvey Fite's viewpoint at this early stage in the development of his art: a stage for placing the monumental carved bluestone statues that filled his mind after Copan. What was to be *Opus 40* was only a secondary consideration.

At the time, Fite's concept of sculpture reflected a critical moment in the entire culture's adjustment to a new way of viewing itself. The form, scale and function of monumental undertakings during his lifetime demanded that his visions as artist be large. His carved statues followed the period's popular theme of representing man as the symbolic master of monumental tasks. Statuary was made large to mount the fronts and tops of triumphal architectural and engineering achievements. *Opus 40* in this context was basically a setting to showcase this grand artistic statement.

However, Fite's artistic intent was to bring something unique to this genre. He purposely retained the stone's dimensionality and mass in the representational content of his sculptures. Citing Mayan art's influence, he declared that "the artist must satisfy the aesthetic sense by working with the limitations of the material." His goal was not to carve an "idealization of a factual reality" from the stone but to blend the representational form he carved with the character of the stone itself. This same interaction also carried through in the arrangement of stones that defined the basic forms of *Opus 40*.

For over twenty years, Harvey Fite paid homage to this concept of the stone's character in his traditional form of sculpture. All the while, he continued to build the stone environment on which he displayed this statuary. A *Look* magazine photo essay of the late 1940s idealizes his country lifestyle in High Woods. In it, *Opus 40* had already attracted the attention of the photographer's eye. So his presence in the art world of the time is of a sculptor already building and inhabiting a special environment. Though he had many gallery shows and awards with his traditional sculpting, the dominant theme of his public image was inseparable from this ever-growing artistic environment of stone.

By 1960, Harvey Fite's concept of the relationship his stone statuary had to the environment he created was beginning to change. By this time, his environment had noticeably out-scaled his figurative sculptures. His sculpture appeared no longer symbolically monumental. The setting and its actual stone had become monumental. So, now in his sixties, he redirected the course of his life's work by removing the statuary from the environment and dedicating himself to transforming the land itself into sculpture. The intuitive sculptural form he had been building for nearly a quarter century thereafter became the central focus of his work. This event established Land Art as a universal theme of artistic interest for the first time.

But he had an even more expansive view planned for this new art form. As he was planning his multi-acre art environment to be a single work of art, he was also developing parallel ways of experiencing the environment that would transcend the physical presence of this sculpture. He was conceptualizing a way to present the quarry itself as a narrative that interpreted the whole history of the people, their culture and the industry of the bluestone material of his artwork. This was to be an integral part of *Opus 40*.

The groundwork for this all began years before. Since he first bought his quarry land in 1938, Fite collected with great and growing interest artifacts from the quarrymen. With his new approach to his art, he began a serious review of these quarrying artifacts. Then he reconstructed a garage into two stories with sheltering overhangs. He arranged this collection on the floor and along every inside and outside wall. He arranged them as aesthetic

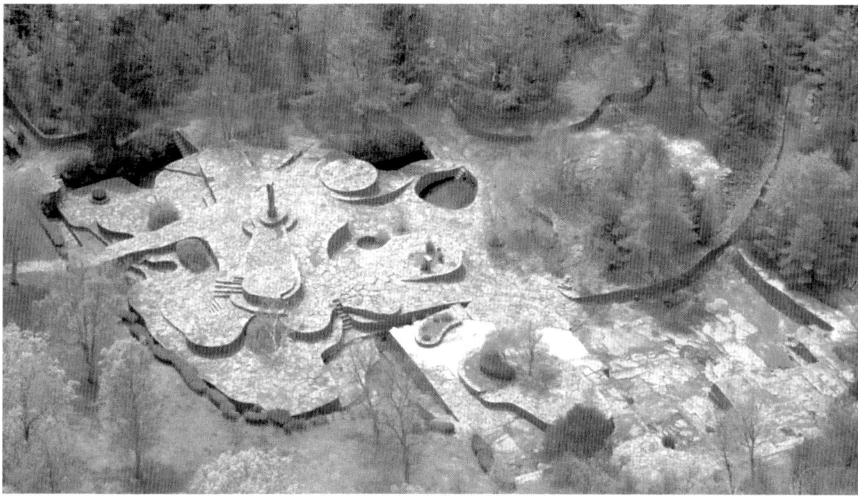

The footprint of *Opus 40* and hundreds of potential bluestone quarry sculpture sites are clearly visible on Internet earth views. *From the author's collection.*

displays with no cataloguing or markings and delighted in giving "tours" where he would describe each item in relation to the life and times of its user. An early black-and-white video exists of one of these tours of what he called his Quarryman's Museum.

To complete this interpretive theme, he cleared what he intended to be a congregating area at the base of the sculpture. In the midst of artistic elements of the site, he uncovered a viewing area for the express purpose of displaying the land as it was before he arrived. What he'd seen was the work of nature—of ancient seas and of more recent glaciers—and also marks in the stone from the work of the quarrymen. In the same way that his Quarryman's Museum honored the life of the workingman, this amphitheater interpreted the life of the stone.

Fite constructed *Opus 40* by hand and only with nineteenth-century quarryman's technology and tools—moving, trimming and setting the stone remnants left to him by the original quarrymen. Fite's narrative of tools, physical work and what the quarry becomes adds to the art through this experience. It suggests *Opus 40* as a work of many long-ago hands and tools sharing the same material space through this work of his hands. The whole work is a collaboration.

This recognition of work of hands is Harvey Fite's individual legacy to the world of art. Those who understand what work of hands means appreciate *Opus 40* in a completely different way from those who approach it for its art history significance or appreciate it on a strictly aesthetic level. But one does not take away from the other. Appreciating the task of building assumes recognition of the quality of what is built. Conversely, appreciation of the quality or cultural significance of what was built presumes that an act of creativity requiring the labors of the artist happened. It is this welding of experiences that Harvey Fite sought through his art and spent his life perfecting.

Had Harvey Fite lived, he would probably have spent his later years enjoying interpreting his beloved site and collection of artifacts. This would have completed his environment. But his intentions are so obvious in the physical presence of his accomplishments that it is this, his spirit, that makes the whole artwork complete. *Opus 40* is the collection, the cleared quarry and the structured Land Art sculpture as a whole.

8

THE HISTORY OF MILL AND WATER RIGHTS OWNERSHIP

Any survey of the history of Saugerties must totally immerse itself in the history of the mills, from their origins to their demise. Without this as a focal point, the other elements have no context. The village of Saugerties could never have been what it was if the mills were never there.

In 1826, Henry Barclay established the paper mill in Saugerties and then transferred ownership of it to his father, Thomas Barclay. He'd turned his attention within the year to establishing the infrastructure of a large community. Thereafter, the Barclay family ran the paper mill and built and ran other investments in Saugerties until Henry Barclay's death in 1851. At that time, all the land and investments of Henry Barclay were sold at an auction except for the paper mill. Management of that was transferred to Joseph B. Sheffield and Norman White, and ownership of this business was transferred to them in 1857. The capital investment that the Barclay family held was retained on the paper mill as mortgages until after the turn of the century and perhaps further. Norman White left in 1867, and in 1869, the business became J.B. Sheffield and Son as William R. Sheffield, who was born in 1847, came of age. The equity stake of the Sheffield family in Saugerties businesses continued to grow from there.

William R. Sheffield grew up in Saugerties and cut his teeth on local politics and its relationship to transportation by forming the Long Dock Company. In the late 1870s, this company did projects such as constructing telegraph lines to the resorts in the Catskill Mountains as part of its business objectives. It also made investments in several Catskill Mountain resort hotels. When W.R.

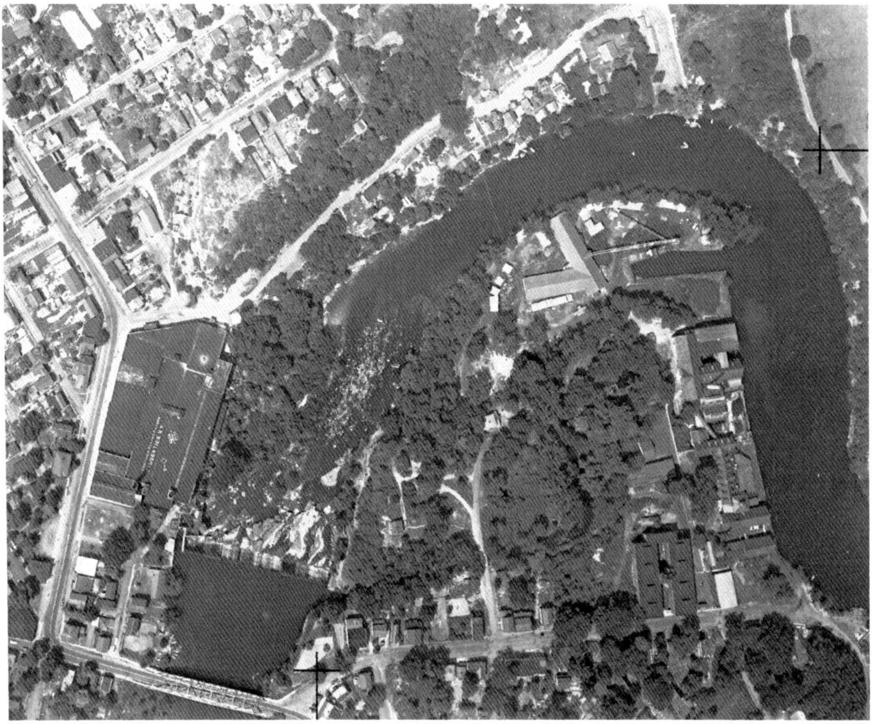

In 1949, the water power infrastructure was still being used by the Martin Cantine Company and the paper mills. *R&L Archive collection.*

Sheffield served as president of the village, he championed improvement of the street and sidewalk systems through the village to benefit visitors and haulers using the Long Dock ferry terminal as the principal link between the established railroad across the river and the new one on the west shore.

By 1882, the Ulster Iron Works and the Sheffield Paper Company, Inc., owned all the lands of the mills on the south side of the Esopus. Before 1887, the iron works had ceased production, and William Mulligan, the owner, sold this property to William R. Sheffield for stock in the Sheffield Paper Company, Inc.

William R. Sheffield then joined with William Parsons to replace the iron works with the Barclay Fibre Company to make pulp from wood fiber, an experimental process at the time. For this expansion, John G. Myers supplied a mortgage on the iron works land to support the construction and equipping of these new facilities, bringing in the first outside capital other than that of the founders.

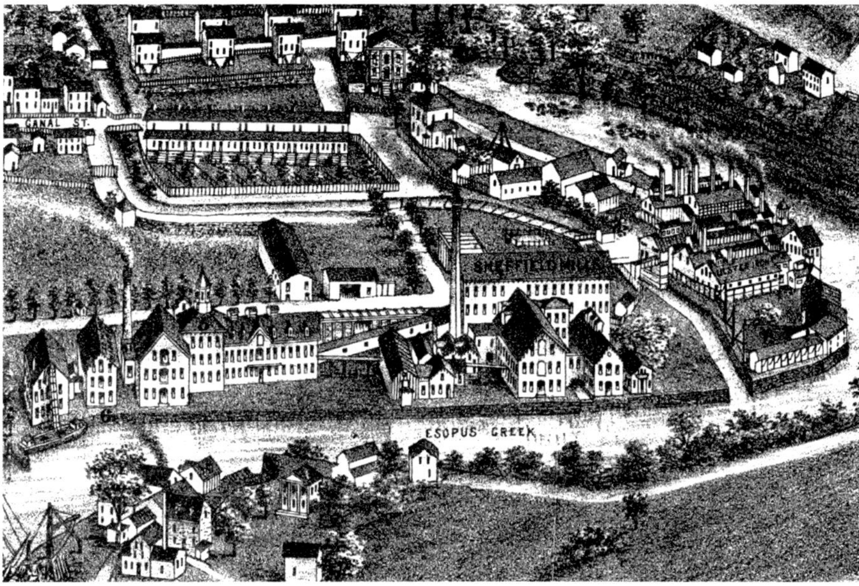

Detail from an 1881 bird's-eye lithograph of the power supply canals after the 1858 agreement that replaced Barclay's original stone dam. *From the author's collection.*

Every construction and operations investment during the nineteenth century was made with private capital. The investors were related by business or family and had continually been hands-on or eyes-on through established relations with Saugerties since its founding. There was no building, road or merchandising business started in this era that was not related to Saugerties' founding industries.

Risk and gain were central to the events of Saugerties history in the nineteenth century. The only remaining nineteenth-century mill still standing in Saugerties, the Mill, is an example of how the risk gambits played out.

Variously known as the blank book factory and the bindery, the Mill was built by Sheffield Paper Company, Inc., and John Q. Preble, Inc., jointly, as the Blank Book Company in 1888 to replace operations lost by the Preble company in a fire the previous year. The date of the partnership could be earlier. Preble, Parson's pulp factory and Sheffield all shared the same address in Manhattan at 10 Thomas Street, so production efficiencies from pulp through paper making and, finally, a finished blank book product, with Preble's business planning to corner that market, may have been in the works for some time.

Half ownership of the Mill was part of the holdings of Sheffield, Inc., when it was forced into bankruptcy in 1889 due to a failure of J.Q. Preble, Inc., and a subsequent cascade in losses from Sheffield's related Chicago sales operations expansion. This bankruptcy was resolved when the bondholders of the Sheffield Family Trust bought the assets of and became mortgage holders for Sheffield Paper, Inc., in 1894, selling all operations to the New York and Pennsylvania Paper Company.

Parsons, whose Barclay Fibre Company was not part of the bankruptcy but had banked on the Sheffield/Preble plan, voluntarily ceased operations separately in 1897 after J.G. Myers had taken possession of the iron mill property in the bankruptcy settlement as compensation for the mortgage he held on the pulp mill. The Sheffield's Long Dock Corporation involvement, a separate development under Sheffield, Inc., went to G.R. Spaulding, a partner in this company, who held a mortgage on its lands.

In the nineteenth century, land was not as important as it is considered today. A mortgage on an improvement on land was the way an investment yielded income and created wealth. In the pre–Civil War years, as Saugerties made its reputation as an industrial center, those associated with investments in any improvement of the land here were considered as wealthy as ground-floor investors in successful technology businesses are today. The relationship to the actual buildings or the land the buildings are on is even today incidental to the capital they represent as places of production.

It is thought that the Barclay family retained their investments in Saugerties well into the mid-twentieth century through the early mortgage debt still owed them by the Sheffield family. That debt listed in the Sheffield, Inc., bankruptcy, as owed to Thomas Barclay and to George Barclay, was likely converted to bonds and assumed by the Sheffield trust. Collateralized debt provided the stable source of income that kept wealthy families going, and bonds were their debt instrument of choice. The wealth of the early Dutch families was not in their large estates up the Hudson but in the small patches of land under the improvements of New York City they owned and leased or sold holding the mortgage.

After 1894, the Sheffield trust was solely interested as a land holder that either leased or was a mortgage holder of the mills it had sold. Barclays and Sheffields played no active part in the actual manufacture of paper but maintained that financial interest. It is that income that helped the Sheffield family carry on a lifestyle typical of the Gilded Age with townhouses in Boston, upper Manhattan and Paris and memberships in the clubs where William R. Sheffield was known as a kingmaker in Republican politics from

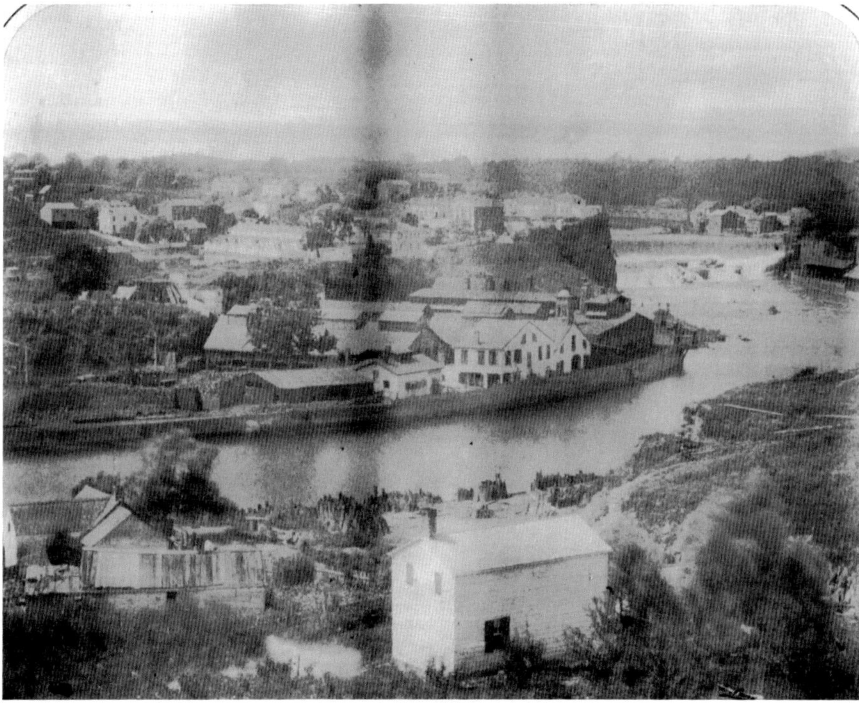

Post–Civil War photograph of the Ulster Iron Works capturing the community built on the slopes of Barclay Heights that supported it. *R&L Archive collection.*

his association as spokesman for the lucrative paper interests and a leading investor in the industry.

The Sheffield Family Trust leased the blank book factory it owned as the Sheffield Manufacturing Company to the Saugerties Manufacturing Company in 1894. Its owners divided the building into bindery operations in the west building and envelope manufacture in the east building. In 1894, the first embossed stamp envelopes under contract for the United States Post Office were made in the east building under a lease. By 1912, the Saugerties Manufacturing Company again occupied the entire Mill with bindery operations and had become the largest maker of the then patented ring binders with spring opening, and its Sterling brand was the most popular packaged filler paper in the country. Their Sterling brand is still famous as the ubiquitous composition book.

F.L. Russell was brought in as manager for the Saugerties Manufacturing Company in 1929, and in 1936 he vacated the buildings and moved all operations to the Martin Cantine Co. Tissue Factory building on Ulster Avenue.

The Mill was leased to Knaust Bros. in 1939. They were large producers of mushrooms and used old factories also in Hudson and Catskill as environments for cultivating mushroom spores that would be taken to limestone caves for growing. In 1941, they bought the property from Henry Hazen Reed, who was said in the documents to be the last remaining trustee of the bondholders of the Sheffield Family Trust. Then, in 1942, Knaust Bros. leased the building to RCA for wartime production. In 1946, they upgraded the heating system for leasing it to General Electric.

In 1953, Knaust Bros. sold the Mill to Northeastern Holdings, which leased it to Ferroxcube through 1964. After that, the building was leased for a few years for poultry production and then sat abandoned until it was converted to senior housing in the late 1990s.

The paper mill probably left the Sheffield trust in 1949 after the estate of Ralph Thompson—heir to Colonel George Thompson, who had purchased the company for the Diamond Mill Paper Company in 1903—sold it to a company called Flavicon, a maker of packaging for the food industry. At this time, mortgages began to be held by banks, and a succession of calls on these mortgages after Flavicon for Ulster Paper Company, the Ulster County Paper Company and the Empire State Paper Company were recorded right up to the late 1960s, when there began a succession of fires in several different buildings. The last known activity in the paper mill was a record of equipment taken on a tax lien. Sometime in the early 1970s, a wrecking ball was taken to the structures and the brick hauled away for fill.

This transition from private to commercial debt after the war was what signaled the decline of innovative startups in Saugerties. The tradition that reserved opportunities and risks to the insiders of an investment community that began a century and a quarter before had even weathered the Great Depression. But it had been weakened by events that also affected the very soul of Saugerties.

All of the first generation of industrialists came to Saugerties for the investment opportunity. They passed this on to a second generation, where Martin Cantine stands alone as being from a pre–Henry Barclay family. His father, Peter Cantine, a lawyer and judge, was from a long line of colonial Ulster County planters. His father's sister's daughter was married to Edwin Gould, the son of the financier Jay Gould. Martin's brother Charles, a lawyer and also a judge, was his partner in starting the Martin Cantine Company. Charles was married to Mary Sheffield, a daughter of J.B. Sheffield. When Mary died when their daughter Agnes was just six, Charles, as guardian, became a trustee in the Sheffield Family Trust.

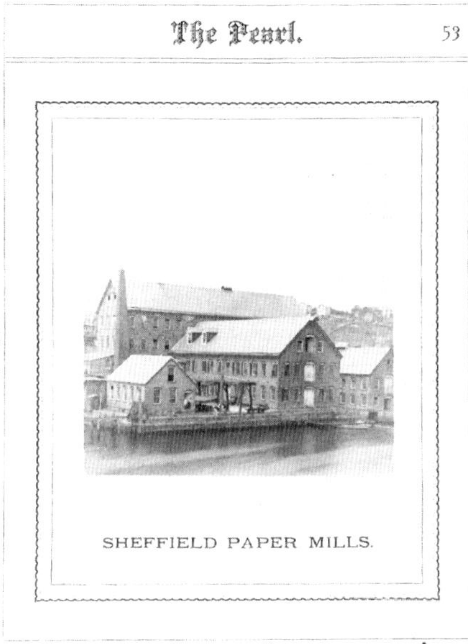

In 1875, Sheffield and Son's new paper mill structures had just replaced Henry Barclay's original mill built in the late 1820s. *Courtesy Audrey Klinkenberg.*

This connection gained Martin Cantine a management training position in 1882 at the Sheffield paper mills when he was just sixteen. He established the Martin Cantine Company in 1888 when he was twenty-two. He placed his factory on the north side of the Esopus on the land that had always been too high to have the advantages of the water for power. He introduced the efficiencies of hydroelectric power to manufacturing there, and the process controls in paper coating he developed placed the company's products in a stable market for nearly eighty years.

Martin Cantine began to involve himself in his family's native connection to the land when he acquired the estate of Mary Pidgeon in its bankruptcy sale of 1906. This was the large farm of the Kiersted family. The Kiersteds had been established in Saugerties for half a century before Henry Barclay arrived and the industries began. Their lands stretched from Main Street at the Kiersted house to where the Cantine field, the high school and the Horseshows in the Sun (HITS) lands are today. This was all called Valley Farm. Martin Cantine lived in the house his father had lived in on the south side of Main Street, the second house east of the Main Street School, on a small rise that on early maps was called Cedar Hill, and looked out over the whole of Valley Farm from there. In his will, he donated the open fields he had always known opposite the school to the Saugerties school board so that there would always be this open view from the school's windows.

When Martin Cantine died in 1936, the Valley Farm was purchased from the estate by one of the companies run by the farm, the Little Sawyer Ice Company. They sold it immediately to Knaust Bros.

In the mid-1950s, the Knaust Bros. created a grand scheme that included a large medical and industrial research campus with a golf course and three-story professional and apartment buildings, along with a technical high school. This was all merged into the village through a residential sub-development they had begun in the late 1940s. It was a very innovative concept for the time, as was their Iron Mountain document storage business in Columbia County. They called this Saugerties plan Farm Industries.

The village had annexed the part of Valley Farm's land designed for sub-development in 1948, permitting the extension of streets, water and sewage. In 1958, the high school component of the Farm Industries plan became part of the school district's consolidation plan. The Cantine complex and the HITS improvements, and everything east to the river across Stroomzeit was also on land dedicated to this plan and, because of various interventions over the years, ended up in their present uses.

The Martin Cantine Company continued under family ownership and management until it was closed in the late 1960s. By that time, its Tissue Company venture had also closed operations in the Ulster Avenue factory and the F.L. Russell Company that shared this building had moved its operations to a new building in the town on King's Highway. Bank mortgages on these mill properties taken by speculators followed the empty buildings until the original factory on South Partition Street burned in 1978. That property

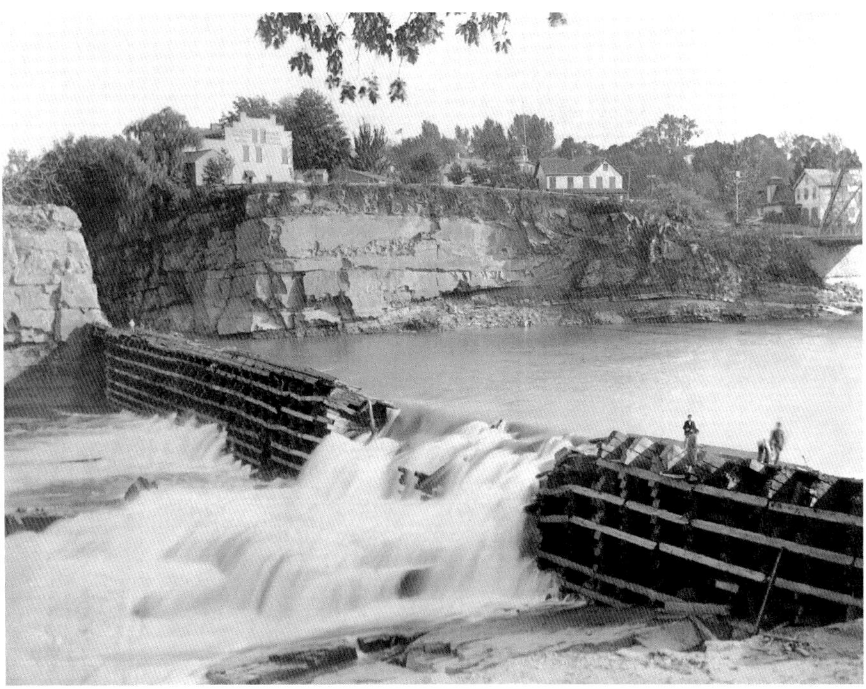

Barclay's 1825 stone dam washed away in 1858 and was replaced by a crib dam until the present concrete one of 1929. *Courtesy Christopher Evers.*

had been foreclosed and was in bank possession at that time, which made the bank the last remaining user of water power in Saugerties. This resulted in the first ever official examination of ownership responsibility for the dam going back to Henry Barclay that had been rebuilt in 1929 by the Martin Cantine Company and the Diamond Mill Paper Company.

The research environment for tracing this responsibility had been so tainted by an attitude that had been brewing over the past twenty years that by the time this was done in 1978, key parts of history were simply ignored in the findings. This greatest of Saugerties' assets had succumbed to the complacency of the times.

However, the history is clearly in the record and is not subject to personal opinion.

In an 1894 legal decision made by Benjamin Coon as referee, Henry Barclay's family's retention of the pond itself was found to have passed to the Sheffield family trust. That decision, in turn, set up a 1903 agreement that resulted in the transfer of the old iron works first rights to the water of the Esopus Creek to the Martin Cantine Company. Both the 1894 and 1903 decisions recognized the Sheffield claim that the bedrock base of the pond extended into the canal's bedrock base, and this gave a continuous right to the natural flow of water to the paper mills as it passed freely to tidewater. This was the flow used to calculate the volume tapped by the canal on the south side of the dam that had previously been divided between the old iron works' historic needs and the paper mill's.

This question of rights started in 1902, when the Martin Cantine Company was going to purchase the old Ulster Iron Works property on the south side of the dam and use its first right to the water to generate electricity for manufacturing at its plant on the north side of the dam. This level of power generation created a need to confirm the historic rights to waters in the canals.

Cantine's plan was to partner with Edwin Gould, who owned the iron works property and use the canal no. 2 flow to run a generator at the pulp mill's turbine. The electricity was to be fed to his plant on the north side of the creek across transmission lines. The land south of Dock Street had been purchased for running these lines to the plant and also into the village. However, the amount of water that could be brought through the rock cut was shown to be insufficient to drive the generating capacity for electrifying the plant and supplying the village and still leave enough for the paper mills.

In the 1903 agreement, there were four parties: the Martin Cantine Company, Edwin Gould, Sheffield Paper Company and Agnes R.L.

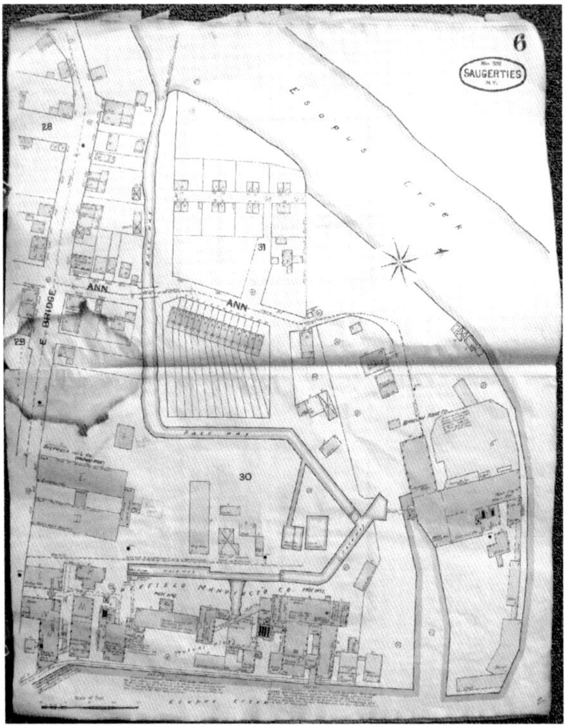

Sanborn insurance maps follow growth in the village from the late 1880s up to the decline of its manufacturing status. *R&L Archive collection.*

Sheffield, representing the bondholders of the family trust. The decisions needed to make the agreement practical were brokered by Judge Charles Davis. Agnes R.L. Sheffield and Edwin Gould were representing contractual agreements they had made to sell to Diamond Mills Paper Company and the Martin Cantine Company, respectively. The agreement involved both water rights and a land transfer resolution.

What was resolved, in essence, was that the dam was divided between electric generation for primary use on the north and for manufacturing as secondary use on the south side. That was done by deeding, for the first time ever, the stream bed between the tidewater and the dam, dividing the respective north and south sides of the dam into two separate ownerships. This involved moving a division of the iron works property and paper mills property that was previously down the middle of the canals in an 1858 agreement in favor of the paper mills' ownership of all canal beds, with canal no. 2 to be capped, filled and totally removed from the map, leaving no water power access to the old iron works site. Joint access to the dam from both the north and south sides was deeded as a ten-foot strip along the south edge of canal no. 1 and along the shoreline of the pond between

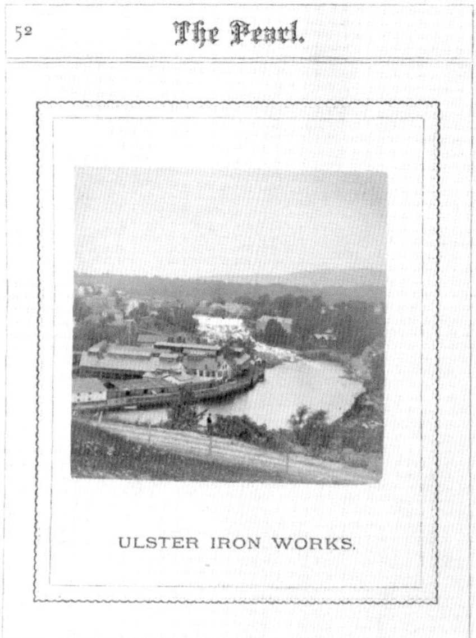

This 1875 photograph follows the tradition of documenting the iron works' picturesque ravine that began in 1831 and continued for a century. *Courtesy Audrey Klinkenberg.*

the bridge and the dam. Right to use these accesses for repair of the dam was granted to each owner.

To this day, as near as can be figured, the four parties of this agreement retain these rights. The power generation right was shared between Cantine and Gould, and the water rights never left the Sheffield trust, which, even though the paper mill was in the process of being sold to the Diamond Mills Paper Company as these negotiations were taking place, always kept some interest in the form of a mortgage or lease to them and each successor, right up to the current era.

These negotiations were under the expert guidance of Judge Charles Davis, arguably the all-time master when it comes to knowledge of legal title to the soil of the village of Saugerties. Sadly, the level of knowledge during the rest of the twentieth century hasn't proven anywhere near as masterful.

It's hardly a wonder since it appears banks were adroitly played by investors in a long series of clever mortgage deals that left so many foreclosures and referee deeds on the record, all ending in the same Sheffield involvements. Ownership has looked like an elaborate shell game since the 1880s. Indeed, there are so many corporate names used in the transfers of the same soil since then that there is no wonder that this confusion about ownership and responsibility had allowed this iconic historic setting to languish in ruin for so long.

The way Judge Charles Davis drew the line in this new era, when water flow was in demand for electricity generation, was to separate water used for factory processes from that used for driving machinery. Placing the first right to the water at the dam itself, where it was unconstrained, and then further constraining the flow at the canal, thereby limiting the secondary rights to not enough water for both power and the water intensive paper making processes, had the effect of endorsing electric or steam-powered machines for factory operations from then on. The fourteen feet of water in the canal above its bed specified in this 1903 agreement left little the ancient mill sites on the south side of the dam could do to expand since the paper making easily used up canal no. 1's full allotment.

In the 1904 laws of the New York state legislature, a final blow to the value of this first right was struck. Section 724 permitted New York City to eventually select a site for its water supply that diverted the flow of the Esopus at its greatest reserve point into the Ashokan reservoir. This seriously handicapped the future of the Barclay dam at Saugerties as a power generation site.

The Village of Saugerties was electrified in the early 1890s. By that time, steam electric generators were common in mills and factory buildings. The use of the electric motor opened up mechanized manufacturing throughout the village, and the insurance maps for 1892 show the symbol for the generator in most of its commercial buildings.

Once the hydroelectric generation had proven itself at the Martin Cantine Company on the north side of the dam, a novelty and crepe paper factory using the Barclay Fibre Company buildings on the south was planned for the power. But by 1912, when production was just starting, the prospects for a steady flow of water had come into question and the Martin Cantine Company began to expand closer to the railroad sidings. In 1914, the Tissue Company factory was built as the first large-scale factory building totally unrelated to water power in Saugerties.

9
THE SOURCES OF HISTORY

Histories are names and events tied to their times but also to those who write them. You begin to relate to history by imagining those people and their stories in their time.

In a letter book of Henry Barclay is copied a response to Moses Y. Beach, who wanted to run a gristmill off Barclay's water power. Barclay's reply is that gristmills do not employ enough workers. He tells Beach the reason for creating the water power was to fill the lots of his village with workers. This exchange took place during the birthing of Saugerties but was just read and interpreted for this writing.

The first mill that Henry Barclay made was an iron works, and within months of his startup, it was sold to Henry Carey, whereupon Henry Barclay exited the iron manufacturing business but continued to use it as a centerpiece of his venture. It is still Barclay's Iron Works in an 1831 William Guy Wall engraving even though it had been for three years by that time the Ulster Iron Works and completely refurbished by John Simmons.

When Barclay's original 1825 stone dam across the Esopus was washed away in 1857 and a wooden one replaced it, Leon Barritt, the most prolific chronicler of his era, was only six years old and Henry Barclay had been dead for six years. Barritt would record the fact that Barclay built the dam and that Sheffield and White—who then owned Barclay's second venture, the paper mill—and the Tuckerman brothers, who then owned the iron works, jointly built the new dam. But Barritt had no idea of what they had agreed to in order to do this—the canals' re-channeling to give the Tuckermans the

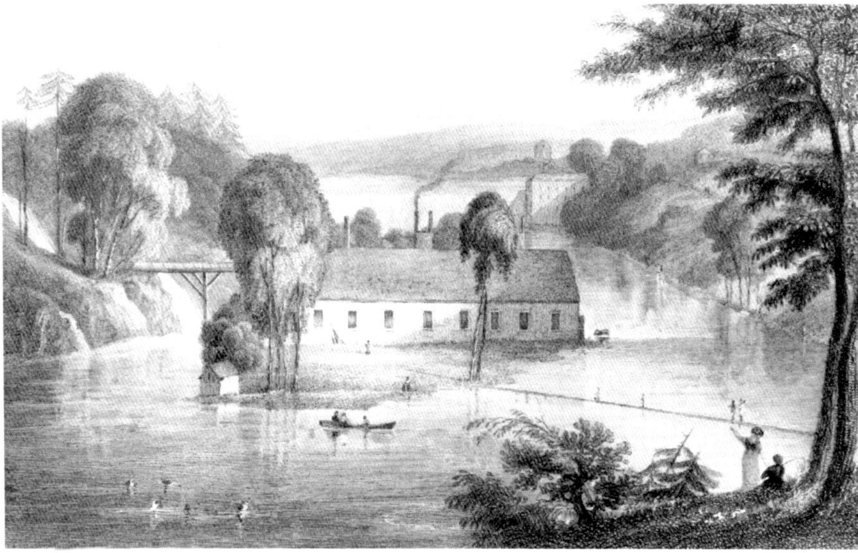

1831 engraving of the first mill built by Henry Barclay showing Livingston's contemporary mill in the background, from a William Guy Wall original. *Author's collection.*

direct flow of the water and the filling in of the reservoir and the paper mill's power supply throttled by a small outlet called canal no. 3. Henry Barclay's plan of using a large reservoir to extend the water of the pond that passed through the rock cut to power many smaller mill sites twenty feet below this reservoir on tidewater had been eclipsed by the success of the Ulster Iron Works and the power demands of its rolling mills. But because this was not included in Barritt's writings, speculation on accuracy of an image of a reservoir on the Barclay maps and the 1851 map of the village of Ulster have gone on for over a century. This was simply not there in 1875 when Barritt was writing.

The surfacing of facts that never appeared in the written sources of our history keep it alive. The Ulster Iron Works is legendary for setting the quality standard for production of high-strength iron. But Ulster Iron is less about that legend than it is about the creation of it. There is little we would be driven to clarify about Henry Barclay, paper manufacturing, the iron works or any of the history of this early era if it were not for what can be read today that was written by Leon Barritt.

To the point, a later writer at the beginning of the twentieth century, Benjamin Myer Brink, did not even try to chronicle the nineteenth century, assuming, of course, these were still current events. He wrote of the Olde

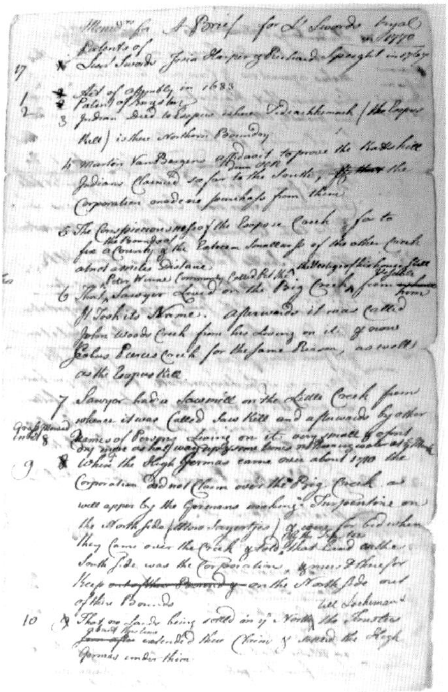

Left: Outside page of a single folded sheet writing down a 1770 timeline of history. *From NYS Library Cockburn Family Collection, Box 10, folder 2.*

Below: Inside of the single folded sheet writing down a 1770 timeline of historic events. *From NYS Library Cockburn Family Collection, Box 10, folder 2.*

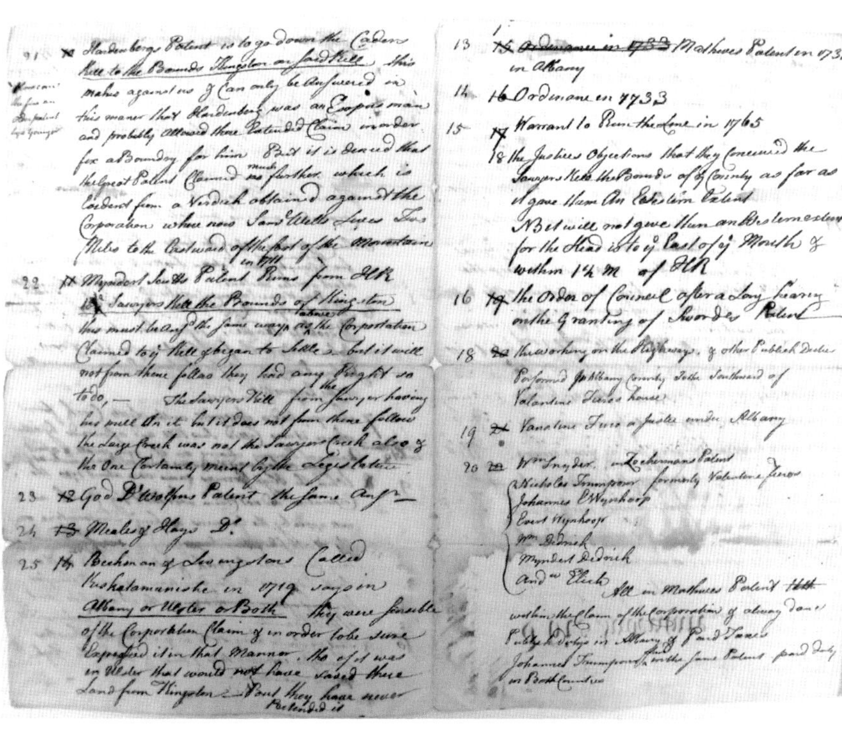

Ulster of colonial times. These Brink and Barritt works are the references that have supported most understandings of the history of Saugerties for the past century. But things continue to surface that their accounts did not have as sources.

The earliest history of Saugerties is a "Memorandum for a brief for Lt. Swords' trial, 1770." It is a single sheet of note paper with a scribbled list of events put into chronological order by adding numbers placed independent of the order of the writing. This lists the names of occupants and ownerships from the first Indian deed up to the time of the writing.

The numbers organize a progression of history supporting a November 6, 1767 Crown grant of two thousand acres overlaying the northern part of the present village of Saugerties and extending west over the Winston Farm and into the hills.

It is a document written by William Cockburn in his capacity as land surveyor. In the eighteenth century, the surveying profession required knowledge of most of the important historical references of the community. Surveyors used their archive of ancient deeds, maps and notes daily for verifying the boundaries they marked.

William Cockburn was not just a local surveyor. He was official surveyor and confidant to Cadwallender Colden, the lieutenant governor of the colony of New York, a recognized intellectual of the period and himself a writer of a history of the Indians. This memorandum used some pretty solid sources from that connection.

Though the references made in the memorandum have already been made clear, this transcription serves to convey a feeling for the understandings of the time, giving a sense of its recollection as its recent past.

Memorandum for a brief for Lt. Swords' trial, 1770

1. Act of Assembly in 1683

2. Patent of Kingston

3. Indian deed to Esopus where Tediachkemach (the Esopus Kill) is the northern boundry [sic]

4. Martin VanBergens affidavit to prove the Kattskill Indians claimed so far down Hudson River to the south that the Corporation made no purchase from them

5. The conspicuousness of the Esopus Creek for to fix the bounds of a County and the extreme smallness of the other creek about a miles distance

6. That Peter Winne commonly called Pet the Sawyer lived on the big creek, a vestage [sic] *of his house still visable* [sic], *from him it took its*

name. Afterward it was called John Woods Creek from his living on it and now Jacobus Pierces Creek for the same reason, as well as the Esopus Kill.
8. Sawyer had a sawmill on the little creek from whence it was called Saw Creek and afterwards by other names of persons living on it, very small and almost dry more as half way up and sometimes no running water at the mouth
9. When High Germans came over about 1710 the Corporation did not claim over the big creek as will appear by the Germans making terpentine [sic] *on the north side (now Sagertjes) and were forbid when they came over the creek and told by the trustees that land on the south side was the Corporations and must therefor keep on the north side out of their bounds*
10. That no lands being settled on the north til Lochermans the trustees about this time extended their claim and settled the High Germans under them
13. Mathews patent in 1731 in Albany
14. Ordinance in 1733
15. Warrant to run the line in 1765. The Justices objections that they concieved [sic] *the Sawyers Kill the bounds of the County as far as it gave them an eastern extent north-south it will not give them a western extent for the head is to the east of the mouth and within 1½ mile of the Hudson River*
16. The order of Council after a long hearing on the granting of Swordes patent
17. Patents of Lieutenant Swards, Josia Harper and Richard Spraight in 1767
18. The working on the highways and other public duties performed in Albany County to the southward of Valantine Fieros house
19. Valantine Fiero a Justice under Albany
20. William Snyder in Lochermans patent. Nicholas Trumpour formerly Valantine Fieros, Johannes Wynkoop, Evert Wynkoop, William Dedrick, Myndert Dedrick, Andrew Elich all in Mathews patent within the claim of the Corporation and alway [sic] *done public duties in Albany and paid taxes. Johannes Trumpour land in the same patent paid duty in both counties*
21. Hardenbergs patent is to go down the "Caderskill to the bounds Kingston on said kill." This makes against us and can only be answered in this manner: that Hardenberg was an Esopusman and probably allowed their extended claim in order fix a boundry for him. But it is denied that the great patent claimed much further which is evident from a verdict obtained against the corporation where now Sam Wells lives two miles to the eastward of the foot of the mountain
(margin note: how can therefor an older patent by a younger)

> *22. Myndert Scutts patent in 1711 runs from Hudson River "at Sawyers Kill the bounds of Kingston" this must be answered the same way as above the Corporation claimed to the kill and began to settle. But it will not from there follow they had any right so to do. The sawyers Kill from the sawyer having his mill on it does not from there follow the large creek was not the sawyers creek also and the one certainly meant by the Legislature*
> *23. Godfried DeWolfens patent the same answer*
> *24. Meales and Hays ditto*
> *25. Beekman and Livingston called Kiskatamaniske in 1719 says in "Albany or Ulster or both" They were sensible of the Corporation claim and in order to be sure expressed it in that manner tho if it was in Ulster that would not have saved their land from Kingston—but they have never pretended it.*

But all the history most familiar to Saugerties comes from *The Pearl*. For over a century, all histories, even Brink's early history, have simply restated Leon Barritt's original words in *The Pearl*.

The Pearl

The Pearl was an eight-page periodical produced in twelve monthly issues during 1875, with pages numbered consecutively, 1 through 96, as a planned Volume 1. *The Pearl* is so rare today that very few have had the opportunity to read its pages before now.

A January 27, 1875 *Kingston Freeman* short article reads:

> **The Saugerties Pearl.**
> *Messrs. Barritt and Jernegan, of Saugerties, have hit upon a plan to make their place attractive, and advertise its advantages to the world. They have started a little eight-page monthly, in which they will depict the objects of interest roundabout their village. Mr. Jernegan furnishing the photographs, three of which will ornament as many pages in each number. Mr. Leon Barritt will furnish the literary portion of the periodical, including descriptions of the pictures. There will be also a page of advertisements. This little periodical is called "The Pearl." It is printed in very elegant style by A. V. Haight, Esq., on heavy tinted-paper, and is the most tasty looking paper ever published in Ulster. It should meet a sale of thousands in Saugerties and in fact the people of the entire county will find it interesting and pleasing.*

Here, for this brief history, is the history of this history writer.

Leon Barritt (1852–1938) led a long, varied and highly productive life as a journalist writer, cartoonist, illustrator, publisher and inventor and later had a rather international reputation.

The first of his Barritt line in the United States, Thomas Barritt, arrived in 1800 with letters of introduction to Thomas Jefferson. He was a Republican forced to flee England for his political views. Thomas Barritt settled in Poughkeepsie and married Mary Henderson of Fishkill in 1811. Their first child, Alice, was born in 1812 and married Benson J. Loosing, the distinguished American historian. Uncle Benson was likely as much Leon's inspiration as a historian as his grandfather was for the sharp political wit Leon Barritt later became famous for.

Thomas Jefferson Barritt, fourth child and third son of the eight children of Thomas and Mary Barritt, was born in Poughkeepsie in 1818. In 1846, after an early life at sea on whalers and freighters, he married Catherine S. Malcolm (Kate). In 1852, T.J. Barritt leased the former Myndert Mynderse tavern on Main Street (facing down Market Street) in Saugerties and purchased it in 1854. He carried on a stationery, news and jewelry business there. During the Civil War, he owned and operated the ferry *Air Line* between Saugerties and Tivoli.

Leon Barritt—the fourth son, third surviving, of T.J. and Kate Barritt—was born in Saugerties in 1852. A Leon Barritt born in 1851 to T.J. and Kate died in 1852, and our Leon was born that same year and given the same name as the deceased brother. (The Library of Congress has an 1851–1938 date in their authorities that has not overcome this confusion. The first Leon is buried in the family plot in Saugerties; our Leon is buried in Brooklyn, New York.)

Leon Barritt contributed news as agent of the *Kingston Freeman* for both Saugerties and Tivoli. His style and his byline are also heavily represented in the town of Saugerties section of Nathaniel Bartlett Sylvester's 1880 compilation of the *History of Ulster County, New York*. *The Pearl* was an entrepreneurial sideline.

Leon Barritt left Saugerties for Boston in 1880 to train and work as an engraver of illustrations. Then, after going to Minnesota for a year after 1882, he returned to Saugerties around 1884 and purchased a house on Elm Street. His contributions and illustrations for *Barritt's Easel*, published for a year in 1884 with his father under T.J. Barritt and Son, were his last works in Saugerties.

Barritt moved from Saugerties, permanently, first to Middletown, to open a stationery business. There, he purchased a half interest in the *Daily Argus* and for a year and a half was its publisher. He sold his interest in the *Argus* in 1889 and then moved to New York City to establish himself first as a contributor of cartoons to the *New York Press*. In 1890, he published a book called *Engravings: How to Establish Their Cost*. After five years with the *Press*, he left to become a general freelance political cartoonist to all the major newspapers in the city.

As a cartoonist, Leon Barritt is best known for his June 29, 1898 *Vim* magazine "The Big Type War of the Yellow Kids" cartoon depicting Joseph Pulitzer and William Randolph Hearst characters dressed as the Yellow Kid arguing over promotion of the Spanish-American War. This gave rise to the term yellow journalism. This political cartoon and the one he drew as commentary on large department stores, making them vampires sucking the life out of small business, are both familiar illustrations still used today to explain the issues of that period in history textbooks.

After producing a popular book on how to draw in 1904 and collaborating with Garrett Serviss in the invention, patenting and production of the Barritt-Serviss Star and Planet Finder in 1906, at the height of his career as an artist, he developed a paralysis in his right hand, losing his ability to draw.

Undeterred, Leon Barritt immediately founded a monthly publication based on his star and planet finder that published the location of stars and planets for each month. Within three years, this became the largest circulation astronomical journal in the world. Leon Barritt's obituary has him still the publisher of his *Monthly Evening Sky Map* when he died at eighty-six on February 1, 1938.

Many newspaper articles on Leon Barritt were written during his later years that are appreciations of his dedication to the historical contexts in his astronomical writings. To the very end, he had lived out the interest in history that is so mature in the work he began in Saugerties.

As an artifact, *The Pearl* itself symbolizes Saugerties as a birthing place of creative innovation. As impressive as *The Pearl* is for the factual contributions in the writing of Leon Barritt, it is equally important as a controlled sampling for a study of early photography. As probably the earliest photo journal application, its directly applied 260-plus developments of the same photo for each issue's page means a digital archive collecting all these photographic prints from all the issues of *The Pearl* is a sampling of the processes of the time that would be available nowhere else.

The Pearl is thus an experience of a historical artifact. But in the content that Leon Barritt left in it and in the *History of Ulster County* and in articles he wrote in newspapers—for instance, promoting the creation of the Saugerties

Long Dock—all the critical information regarded as containing the most accurate content for a history of Saugerties is readily available.

Barritt reports on the testing that defined the quality standard of Ulster Iron. He tells of Barclay's original paper mill burning and then how many Washburn bricks Sheffield used to rebuild it. Details of the processing of the iron and the paper are given as part of the description of *The Pearl*'s period photos of the mills. Everything one needs to know about Saugerties before 1880 had been surveyed by Leon Barritt.

10

A HISTORICAL PERSPECTIVE

Resorts are where people came to enjoy the surroundings and the society. Home has a different feeling. The security and comfort of a place of shelter or socialization has little relation to the feeling of home. That feeling centers on an all-encompassing sense that sharing the best of what a place means between all that hold this same feeling in common is possible.

There are many who gravitated to Saugerties who recognized this primal quest in one another. Of all those who grasped this true north as an element of early Saugerties, only Morris Rosenblum's forensic interests touched on the areas and caused the changes and left the insights that today define a Saugerties that is truly home.

Six years after his law practice was firmly established, the country entered into World War II, and Morris enlisted in the army. For four years, he managed this law practice by mail while in the Pacific acting as adjutant in military affairs and as analyst in intelligence matters. These intelligence activities involved aerial photography. He developed a love of that point of view and brought back with him a camera called a K-24.

Morris had embraced a highly specialized way of using photography in the war. This mission was to confirm that surveys and maps matched what was presently in photographs of the same space. Before the war, Morris had begun to collect land development records, and on his return these wartime activities inspired him to broaden this interest into a highly comprehensive collection to match this interest in aerial photos. He

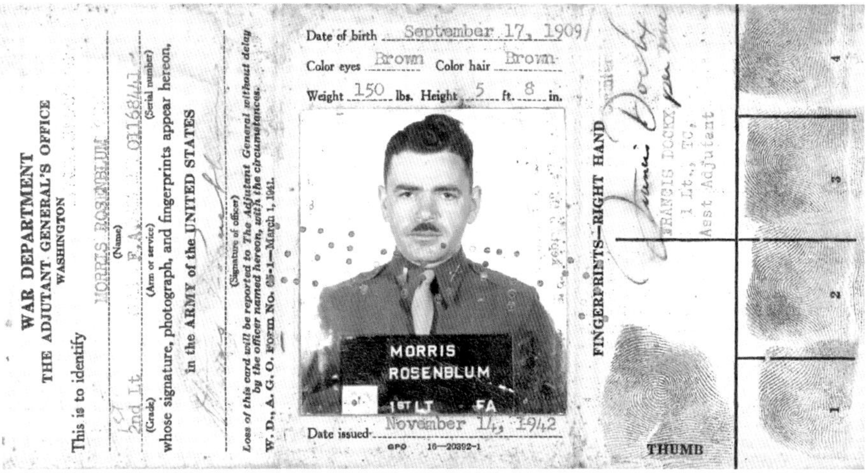

Morris Rosenblum left his law practice to enlist and returned with training that added significantly to our view of Saugerties history. *R&L Archive collection.*

wanted to grasp history in the lanes and hedgerows on historical surveys and maps that the postwar aerial photographs he took showed him.

When Morris left for the war, there were plans for building the Thruway. To Morris, the Thruway was an indicator. The initial nine-mile strip that would inaugurate the thruway concept was being put in Saugerties because this was the ideal place to show off the construction of a high-speed roadway. Miles of arrow-straight reaches that had guided the course of roads for centuries made it obvious that the Thruway would follow a path through here in its course across the state. Its start had to wait until after war ended and enough concrete and steel were once more available, but the economies and efficiencies found here—cement factories, railroad sidings and tidewater facilities within a mile of these perfect landforms—made the early start and progress needed to demonstrate its construction inevitable here.

Morris was a motor enthusiast and had done many cross-country tours in the 1930s. He greatly anticipated the promise of this high-speed highway whose course had already been added to maps. An early public relations identity as the Catskills Thruway was on Morris's mind throughout the war years. Rail and steamboat transportation had helped build the well-known boardinghouse and resort destination that had always been a second-line economy for Saugerties. This relationship to the population of the big city needed little explanation for promoting the idea of a road to rapidly reach a vacationland. The Thruway was marketed as something that would make this place more exciting and easier to reach than ever, and that was the future he spent the war thinking of.

Speed was experienced in air travel and expressed in the aerodynamic design of automobiles. Speed was an engineering challenge for road surface materials and developing the structure of roadbeds. At midcentury, this was the everyman experience of technical knowhow. The practical tests of an actual road with its access ramps and entry and exit to rest areas that were happening here after the war offered realities to match everyone's imagination. As many would be attracted for testing their hand at speed as for speeding to this vacationland.

But speed was a message that captivated a broader area of interest. The Thruway represented something else once this speed was experienced.

During the war, a new industry had begun to grow in this region. Radio Corporation of America (RCA) and now General Electric had been in Saugerties, and IBM was on the other side of the river to the south. This suggested that the two sides of the river would unify into one large electronics-manufacturing region. The Thruway had become a magnet in its symbolic matching of speed to the efficiencies electronics businesses identified with their products.

In the time between the end of the war when the first grading began and a decade later when the Thruway had been completed to the new bridge crossing the Hudson, Morris used the keenest skills he had honed in the war to anticipate how a large industrial campus focused on the research, development and manufacture of the new concept of the computer and dozens of support businesses feeding components into this new industry from places that reached it by the three entrances of the Thruway's short initial twenty-mile length would create feeder communities for the large numbers directly and indirectly employed by these places. He analyzed the intelligence as new homes began to line the roadways radiating from these three entrances, banding this Thruway stretch into a potential artery for suburban residential development.

This cultural aspect of the Thruway is what inspired Morris to initiate events that would resonate throughout the next half century. His intention at first was to make knowledgeable decisions. The principle effect, however, was to demonstrate how the institutional memory here—of enterprise, industry and settlement—was unprepared to cope with what new realities were presenting. Deep down, this place had been primed from the bedrock-solid history Morris recognized to expect a process of housing, then manufacturing facilities and, finally, the centers of commerce that followed innovation. That centuries-old pattern was to be broken this time, and what Morris ended up with was not quite what he expected.

Morris originally arrived here in his mid-twenties at a time when bridges backward into history could still furnish a perspective on the transcendent qualities and continuing presence of tradition. He came in 1935 to resolve some historic relations between local real estate and manufacturing properties that were involved in corporate settlements and debt entanglements. The complex lineage of those who summered here was the target of his interest.

What he found here was a resource whose role was insulating this place from the impact of an otherwise faltering economy, and this intrigued him. This resource was essentially the visitors who arrived in Saugerties annually out of tradition, opening their country homes and welcoming their seasonal guests. They were also those who took up residence in former estates converted to board for the summer those who once had their own summer home here but were now reduced to slightly lessened means.

For the past half century, the New York townhouses had been emptying every summer to fill destinations such as these. This was a social function that did not change just because current means were diminished. Regardless of their circumstances, these families were required to be "in residence" here. It was a social duty.

These were the children, grandchildren, nieces and nephews and their families whose seasonal occupancy in Saugerties was regarded as an obligation passed down to them from a founding generation. Their residences were the estates of Brightbank, Clifton, Clovelea, Stroomzeit and the once great estates that retained their identities as Inglewood, Oak Ledge and others that now catered to the familiar but presently estate-less "refined classes" in these great houses that were now referred to as resorts. This annual ritual was not just a retreat from the city and summer heat. It was a reminder of their roots in a golden age when this place was the seat of their family identity.

Personal wealth here had long been expressed by maintaining scenic views over finely kept grounds cropped by resident herds of sheep in the time before the lawnmower and now by the equipment of their resident groundskeepers. These started out as the local seats of the local manufacturing and merchant establishment whose main residences were in upper Manhattan or Brooklyn. In the "season," these became a show of a proprietor's presence in civic affairs where their volunteer reins of the government, church councils and bank boards were requisite parts of their local business relations.

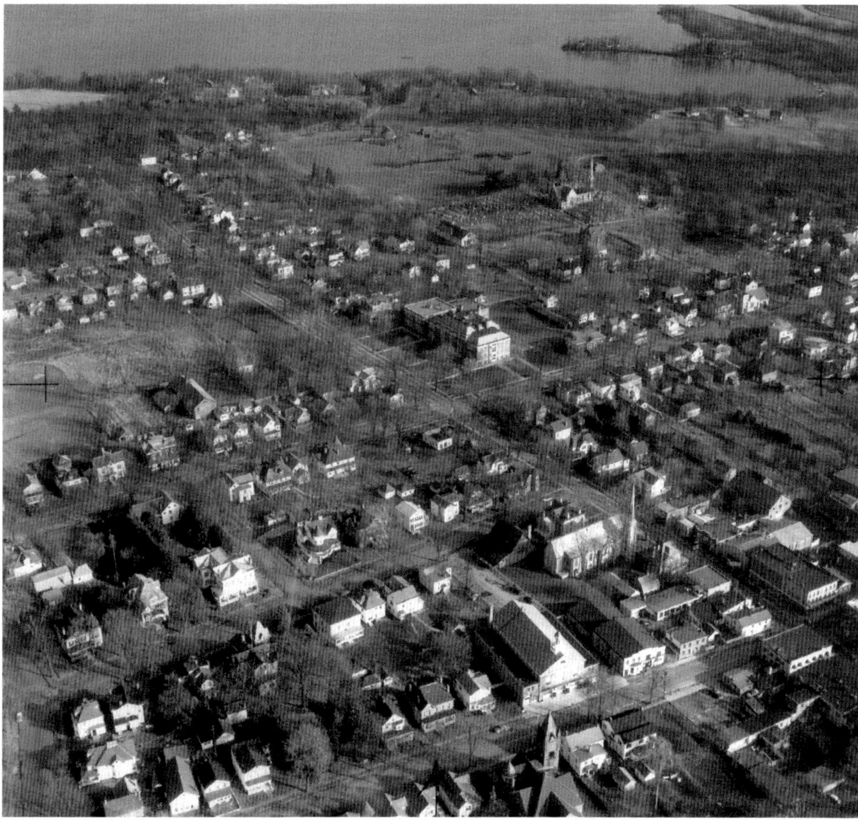

Morris Rosenblum's K-24 aerial surveillance camera captured the corner of Washington Avenue and Main Street looking east in 1955. *R&L Archive collection.*

Later, many of these estate settings were purchased by the even more well-to-do, and many recreational and cultural facilities were financed by them to show that their private appreciation of nature's beauty was accompanied by a love of public settings where they could show off their families and keep their visitors amused with the summer socials they organized.

The sharing of the private lawn, park and trail facilities between these large estates was the predecessor of the many local recreational benefits that grew to support the destination promotions of the ever-expanding list of local resorts and summer boardinghouses. Right up to midcentury, the support of this function made up a sizable indirect economy. Each one depended on a staff of indoor and outdoor help throughout the year. A sign that this economy was on the decline was that it became a curiosity to speculate upon as to when competitive employment opportunities the Thruway brought and the large national employers its attraction drew would begin to divert this local workforce.

For ten or more generations, this place had regarded employment as a demand opportunity—for the farm harvests, the ice harvest, the months when quarrying was practical or when the river was open—and the work related to summer visitors followed this familiar pattern.

To this day, this type of employment still holds on here, but ironically, the tradition of associating seasonal visitors and weekend homeowners with the luxuriant accommodations of the steamboat that is "boat people" in their vocabulary has been formed into a vernacular term for tourists and spoken disparagingly now by those who benefit most from this employment.

Morris knew well that the contacts that could be made by being where this quality of people amused and recreated presented opportunities that would otherwise be difficult to find in the Depression times of the 1930s. The currently fragile rights and tastes of this privileged group would be a full-time occupation for one capable of steering a course through the fragile reality of the fleeting past they represented.

During these years, there was a particularly strong match between the pride in the industrial heritage that built Saugerties and a contemporary emphasis on the heroic industrial landscape artists chose as themes for their work. The cultural values both the founding families of Saugerties and artists brought from their city homes led to diversionary visits to the neighboring art colony of Woodstock, where receptivity to their patronage paid homage to this legacy. During these lean years, this was one of the few ways they could sustain their connection to manufacturing and reinforce that identity while in Saugerties.

The cosmopolitan interests Morris had acquired in his college and early working years in New York City, as well as the original purpose of his introduction, made him highly acceptable company in these circles. His abiding interest in knowing the history that drove their affairs brought him into their conversations. Their common history was the vocabulary and connective tissue that guided all their activities, and being included in their personal conversations brought an understanding of the cultural trappings and general familiarities they shared.

Totally unlike the litanies of common families, their tales delved into a more comprehensive drama as the character of their conversation passed the test of generations of investigation, analysis and introspection. Every season, their discussions had to conclude a formal account of precedents that could presage when the next change was imminent. So before every

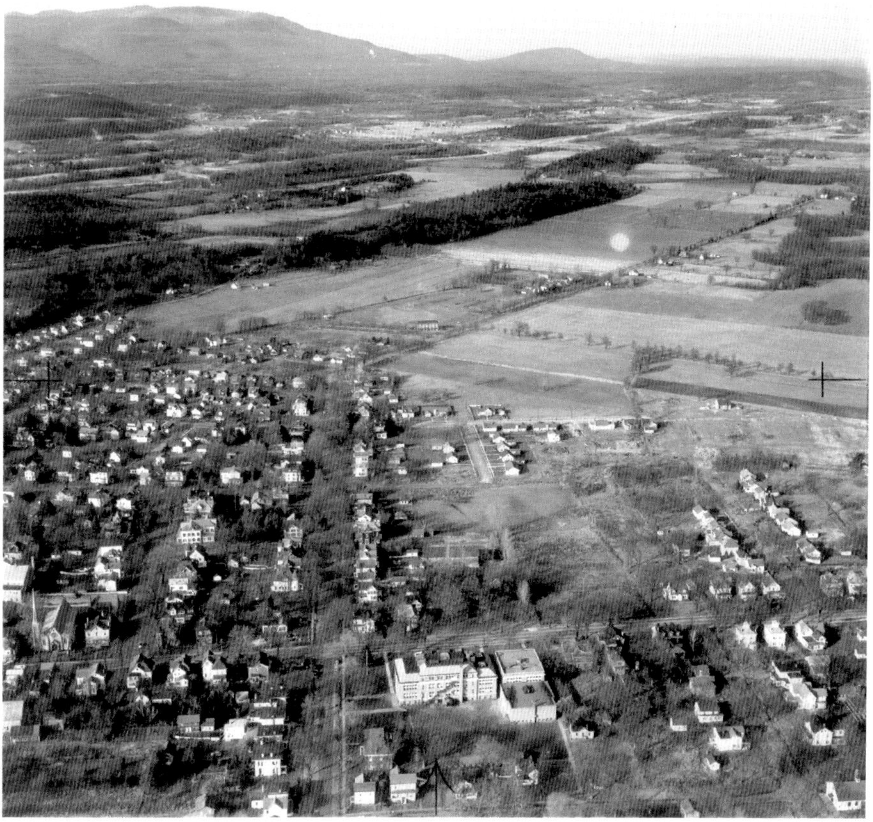

Morris Rosenblum's K-24 aerial surveillance camera captured the corner of Washington Avenue and Main Street looking north in 1955. *R&L Archive collection.*

new social age, the past was made a historical age they all agreed to recall. This custom of perpetuated identity influenced Morris greatly.

These remembrances evolved out of formal information sources—physical collections of family heirlooms that enshrined proof of the special historical times for those who remembered. The credibility of a memory was verified through reference material made up of deeds, ledgers, contracts, surveys, letter books and family Bibles—records spanning one hundred years. These were the province of the family elders or, in the fractious family, the counselor. Permission to witness any of these articles was a sign of deference since belief in their significance was expected.

Morris became the counselor, and from that association in the prewar years, he was one of the few who retained the confidence of these families

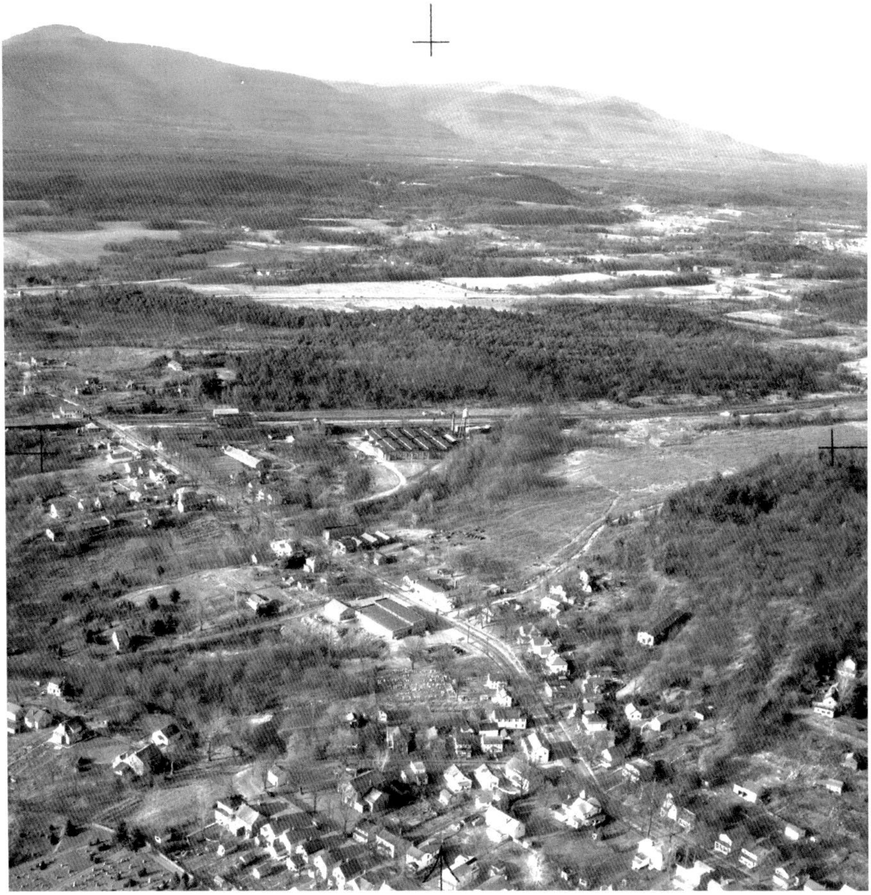

Morris Rosenblum's K-24 aerial surveillance camera captured Ulster Avenue looking west to the Winston Farm and Catskill escarpment in 1955. *R&L Archive collection.*

in the later years when increasingly there was little recognition of the significance of their presence in the new population that rapidly grew in Saugerties after the war.

The duality of his foresight as witness to the encroachment of a future course of land use and his parallel sympathy for a history that no longer had a place for these estates ironically favored him to preside over their sale and oversee breaking them into parcels as their heirloom history collections were entrusted to him to be kept as the final testament when this mainstay of Saugerties departed.

Within the second decade after the Thruway opened, Morris was instrumental in making three of the larger holdings into housing developments, dividing another so the high school campus could be placed there and negotiating retention of the largest estate as a trophy possession for a careless investor that allowed the mansion and other structures to rot.

As the subdivisions and chain store parking lots took over once great lawns and estate lands, there was not one tearful farewell. By that time, Morris, too, was gone, and recognition of these landmarks had twice been removed from memory as the past half century witnessed their first replacements age to be themselves replaced. With all physical presence erased, the "heritage" those here for generations show off as their rite of passage is found only in the memory of those newly arrived with the Thruway, to whom suburbanization and urban renewal is their only historic identity.

EPILOGUE

All meaning is lost to the obvious here. Things just work too well: a pasture has just the right number of springs for its herds; a barrier ledge sheds its rock to make a perfect incline for passage; waterfalls are above the ideal shelter for a hunter's perch; hills just want to glow in the morning and embrace the day at its close in a way that passes along every light the eye can behold.

There is no point in naming these blessings when they never had to be wished for and the imagination never had to conceive a place not this. One simply ignores this presence among all that obviousness. The reality is deftly dimmed in the enigmatic shade of perpetually replenished moments, and the possessors of all this good fortune pass unaware of any cause or past, believing only in the promise of their present. It is all just accepted as the ordinary state of being.

But *being* here is posed as a grand conundrum: in a place such as this where all seems inevitable, a presence still challenges the resilience of spirit and opens the mind to an elusive, veiled reminder of events of a past.

Advancements—innovations—poised to ready some ultimate disruption continually surface in a record of vision and inspiration that seems to spring from a source within this inclusive, subtle accord. In art, merchandising, industry, manufacturing, product development, music, government and most all other endeavors, creativity has entered the narrative. Traces of this start with the first publication of a written record of this place nearly four centuries ago and continue today.

There is a persistent presence in the records that form the history of this place. Though each sees it differently in a different passage of time, the history as a whole follows some prescribed flow where its past moments are echoed in its present—a transcendental history of consequential events, reverberating in waves of importance, mystically verifying that this presence directs it.

A string of recorded instances carries a consistent message that, throughout the whole span of this history, yields little evidence that any difference has ever existed between what the creators of the ideas of their time embraced as inspiration and what those of another past answering to the persuasions of their own time found they needed. From the record's point of view, the actors are all performing the same pilgrimage dance as in many, many other incarnations of the same past here. There is a redundancy that makes the inevitability of an outcome today the same as at least what should be expected from just taking the time to grasp this history.

The events of this history simply happen here because being here makes this the right place for them to happen. That is what the record implies, and that explains why there has been a break in this history ever since this presence stood revealed.

A transition has been in place ever since a record, in a literal sense, of the composition of this place, in aerial photography—on film—was created. These photographs taken over half a century ago reflect a point of view that the photographer holds as a personal perspective on the very presence that is inspiring him. Implicit in the light and time of day of these creations is the character of the omniscient presence of place—something sensed, alluded to—for so long in this history…what the history was not supposed to reveal.

These photographs displayed the purest realization of every way this presence had tempted creative perception for all this time. Portraits of this place have been made as far back as human awareness of it have left records, and each time, these renderings' attempts at capturing that ethereal attraction just invited more to try. This aerial concept shook the foundation of this age-old compact with a creative preoccupation for envisioning an identity for this presence.

The creative resources that had always bridged between the present era and a lucid awareness of its precedents had built a rich tradition of written history. That is what was always meant to perpetuate this long tradition of benign, watchful interest in an absolute presence. This, now, when mated with the technological potential of the current era, is in danger of becoming lost as a pornography of virtual likeness.

The aerial view, as a measure of physical change over time, hearkened toward a change from the personal meditations of the artist to the invasive obvious. In the standpoint that digital views of the earth convey today—impersonal observations that mechanically capture arbitrary features, even the forced links to street-level views—viewers are bound to the trivial and banal scenes of common life. These photographic images thus inevitably lead to the objectification of the inspirational qualities this presence once addressed with impunity.

Thus this transition unfolded, as a disruption, serving up a break in this history, ironically in a spirit of development carried in the person of the very creator of the cathartic photographs that foretold it.

To summarize, first, a half century ago, the population here doubled in a two-decade burst of suburbanization. These numbers deserted the long-standing allegiances as their commuting abandoned the century-old community base. Then stability suffered as the new arrivals were disinclined to identify with a structure whose affairs had always been under the guidance of the local manufacturing, business and merchant class, the wisdom of their owners always providing the officers of the government, the boards of the banks and for guiding the schools and the church congregations. So a pedestrian sense of self set in to socially level the playing field and civic involvement disintegrated as disinterest became the dominant attitude. That drove every established tradition into decline and diluted the identity of this place to where it could have been any place. In short, nearly every prompt for living memory of what preceded the present was erased by almost three generations of those embedded with this disinterest.

Today, an interest in local identity is positioned to reboot awareness of this dormant presence. The most recent quarter century has seen this in a pride in historic structures that started with recognition of the significance of the old commercial district's buildings. The *historic* brand reached the traditional base as one farm became a National Register homestead and another became a venue for horse shows. In between, stone houses gained renewed respect, a lighthouse was restored, parks attracted far more than local interest, a weekend in August became enshrined in music legend, the mountainside became designated "wild wilderness" and the riverfront got "scenic significance" status.

That has all merged into a single path, now tipping the scale toward a new surge in building that's transforming the once farmed and quarried but now overgrown and wooded countryside into hundreds of insular objectifications of urban escape fantasies. Cumulatively, this gentrification of the countryside is on its way toward consuming an amount of land nearly equal to all the suburban development that came before it.

The earth's aerial images are progressively growing into a stage for counting the remote clearings that frame these getaways—a viewing pastime that has captured the attention of the curious and inspired the imagination of these newest arrivals who embrace the concept that their cloistered retreats fulfill the same desire for home ownership and new technology jobs that brought the disruptive choices of unnatural geometry they share equally in the same landscape, in this great virtual earth view.

The affection the latest arrivals feel in their yearnings for the ideal of a local society, locally available resources, a local heritage and culture—all concepts made so attractive in the past quarter century's revelation of historic amenities that brought them here—is a counterforce to the diffused sensitivities that preceded them. They believe sincerely that they are destined to bring in the next phase of the future history of this place.

The focus on knowing the past is now renewed. But if there is one message that history has, it is that no detail of its progression can be dismissed. There are hidden gifts to be realized in the recent past that are exactly the same as those that previous eras grew from, regardless of how unbeneficial they may have appeared in their own time. Knowing the "now" first helps for knowing its origins. The present state of being will be revealed in relation to that.

BIBLIOGRAPHY

Support for the themes presented in this work are from information on the local physical and cultural environment found, in addition to this bibliography of publications, in period handwritten and typewritten documents written in the times of this history and only recently made accessible through digital transcriptions, as well as in the Optical Character Reader searches of *New York World*, *Kingston Freeman*, *Brooklyn Eagle*, *New York Sun*, *New York Times* and dozens of other newspapers, dating back as far as 1800, available from the Internet at fultonhistory.com.

Barker, Kim. *Harvey Fite's Sculptural Landscape Opus 40: A History and Preservation Plan*. Chicago: Art Institute of Chicago, 2005.

Barritt, Leon, and Edward Jernegan. *The Pearl*. Saugerties, NY: Barritt and Jernegan, 1875.

Brandt, Clare. *An American Aristocracy: The Livingstons*. New York: Doubleday & Company, 1986.

Brink, Benjamin Myer. *Early History of Saugerties, 1600–1825*. Kingston, NY: R.W. Anderson and Son, 1902.

Burrows, Edwin G., and Mike Wallace. *Gotham—A History of New York City to 1898*. New York: Oxford University Press, 1999.

Dickinson, Harold T. *Quarries of Bluestone and Other Sandstones in the Upper Devonian of New York State*. University of the State New York, Bulletin 61, New York State Museum, March 1903, Albany.

Divine, Joseph. *The Colden Family of Early America*. Coldengham, NY: Coldengham Preservation and Historical Society, 2011.

Eights, James. "Notes of a Pedestrian." *Zodiac* (Albany, NY), January 1836.

Evers, Alf. *The Catskills: From Wilderness to Woodstock*. Garden City, NJ: Doubleday & Co., 1972.

Mead, Daniel Webster. *Water Power Engineering*. New York: McGraw Publishing Co., 1908.

Morris, Richard B., ed. *Encyclopedia of American History*. New York: Harper & Brothers, 1953.

Osgood, Herbert R. *The American Colonies in the Seventeenth Century: Volume II, The Chartered Colonies. Beginnings of Self-Government*. New York: MacMillan Company, 1905.

Rhoads, William B. *Ulster County, New York: The Architectural History & Guide*. Delmar, NY: Black Dome Press, 2011.

Rich, John Lyon. *Glacial Geology of the Catskills*. University of the State New York, Bulletin 299, New York State Museum, December 1934, Albany.

Ruedemann, Rudolf. *Cambrian and Ordovician Geology of the Catskill Quadrangle*. University of the State New York, Bulletin 331, New York State Museum, December 1942, Albany.

Schoonmaker, Marius. *The History of Kingston, New York*. New York: Burr Printing House, 1888.

Sylvester, Nathaniel Bartlett. *History of Ulster County, New York*. Philadelphia: Everts and Peck, 1880.

Titus, Robert. *The Catskills in the Ice Age*. Fleischmanns, NY: Purple Mountain Press, 2003.

Weeks, Lyman Horace. *A History of Paper-Manufacturing in the United States, 1690–1916*. New York: Lockwood Trade Journal Company, 1916.

INDEX

H

I

J

K

L

ABOUT THE AUTHOR

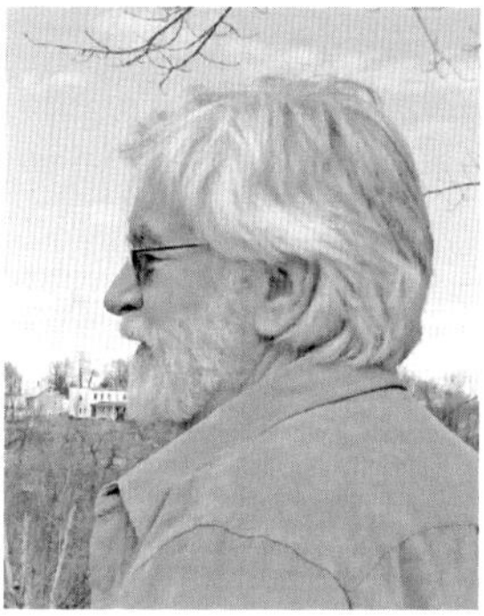

Michael Sullivan Smith is a person with many interests. He is currently busying himself as a sculptor, hand building an earthart artwork. The cultural and physical environments of this sculpture are responsible for his interest in local history. Forty-plus years ago, his fascination with Sir Kenneth Clark's approach to his great work *Civilization* brought him to teach art history from the personal perspective, and this approach has continued throughout a life of cultural and creative discoveries from whence came three patents and four business ventures and the ongoing presence of a broad range of art projects using every variety of media available to the studio arts and the Internet. He retired from his business ventures to devote himself to fine art a decade and a half ago and over that time has been advocating for historic preservation to enlighten his community on the cultural assets that have been lost as a way of protecting the legacy of his own creations. He writes works on local history that are often found in the area newspapers and is a founding member of the Town of Saugerties Historic Preservation Commission. His digital History Atlas of Saugerties places a more chronological history than this brief history in the context of an interactive research environment and can be found in its own computer in the Saugerties Public Library. His mission in writing this book is to inform real writers of a real history-rich place worthy of sinking their talents into for creating their own stories about Saugerties. This brief history is more about the presence of a place where someday the drama of a historical novel will find an author. More on his art projects and his views on the history of Saugerties can be found on his website greatknot.com.